In this book Edmond Malinvaud intends to serve the theory of economic policy. Drawing on his experience as a macroeconomic theorist, policy adviser, and government statistician, he considers the problems associated with diagnosing unemployment, paying attention to the role of forecasting. The analytical framework and the policy environment in which diagnosis occurs are also highlighted.

The book begins by examining the role of economists as theorists and expert advisers. The methodological choices that expert advisers confront, and the political context in which they operate, are carefully set out, as is the case for the implementation of active macroeconomic policies in modern market economies. In this context the nature of economic projections and the ethics of advising are both considered.

Professor Malinvaud has devoted a great deal of his professional career to diagnosing the macroeconomic causes of unemployment. In the final chapters of the book he outlines the difficulties forecasters face in distinguishing between frictional and disequilibrium unemployment. The impact of changes in the demand for labour on medium-term unemployment trends are assessed by focusing in particular on the effect of real wages on investment and employment.

Diagnosing unemployment

Federico Caffé Lectures

This series of annual lectures was initiated to honour the memory of Federico Caffé. They are jointly sponsored by the Department of Public Economics at the University of Rome, where Caffé held a chair from 1959 to 1987, and the Bank of Italy, where he served for many years as an adviser. The publication of the lectures will provide a vehicle for leading scholars in the economics profession, and for the interested general reader, to reflect on the pressing economic and social issues of the times.

Diagnosing unemployment

Edmond Malinvaud
Collège de France, Paris

CAMBRIDGE
UNIVERSITY PRESS

331.137
M25d

Published by the Press Syndicate of the University of Cambridge
The Pitt Building, Trumpington Street, Cambridge CB2 1RP
40 West 20th Street, New York, NY 10011-4211, USA
10 Stamford Road, Oakleigh, Melbourne 3166, Australia

First published 1994

Printed in Great Britain at the University Press, Cambridge

A catalogue record for this book is available from the British Library

Library of Congress cataloguing in publication data applied for

ISBN 0 521 44533 7 hardback

CE

Contents

Preface to the Caffé Lectures 1990

It is an honour to open this series of lectures that the University La Sapienza has decided to devote to the memory of Federico Caffé who, from 1959 to 1987, was professor of economic and financial policy at the department of public economics. Others will describe more accurately the personality, the life, the role and the scientific contributions of Professor Caffé. But I want to record here the sympathy that I feel for someone who lived through almost the same historical period as I did, preceding me only by nine years, who had often to reflect on the same issues as I had to and whose sentiments I certainly shared in many cases.

Federico Caffé was not only an academic devoted to his teaching but also a man involved in the actual problems of the time. He was a long-time influential collaborator of the Bank of Italy and he frequently took part in public debates about Italian economic policy choices.

Federico Caffé was a Keynesian. He took Keynesianism neither as an orthodoxy nor as the belief in a set of precepts ready to be used independently of historical events, but as an 'uncompleted intellectual revolution'. The *General Theory* not only provided an analytical system, but also showed how public intervention had a fundamental function in the conduct of the economy. About the necessity of this function Professor Caffé never had any doubt, notwithstanding the questioning by some theoreticians during the last two decades.

Federico Caffé as a humanist was deeply concerned by the various economic malfunctionings in our world. He could not accept that unemployment, inequity in income distribution or high real interest rates be viewed only as unavoidable consequences of market equilibrium. He knew that the economy was for 'the service of man' and that social objectives required the intervention of the welfare state (see in particular his last publication, *In difesa del 'Welfare state': soggi di politica economica*, Rosenberge Sellier, Turin, 1986).

It is proper for these lectures to deal with one among the various subjects that concerned Professor Caffé, but also with one subject about which the lecturer may have something significant to say that has not already been published elsewhere. The diagnosis that experts have to produce in order to enlighten the choice of economic policy seems to me to deserve our attention on this occasion. Dealing with this subject I shall try to pay a proper tribute to the man we are honouring today.

Acknowledgements

The author would like to thank the publishers of the following articles for their kind permission to reprint them in this book.

Chapter 2: Revised extracts from 'Analyse et prévision: leurs rôles respectifs dans la maîtrise de nos destins', *International Journal of Forecasting* 3 (1987), pp. 187–94.

Chapter 3: Delatour Lecture: 'From statistics to projections', published in French in *Bulletin de l'Institut International de Statistique* (46th session), Tokyo, 1987.

Chapter 5: 'La courbe de Beveridge' in AFSE (1987), *Flexibilité, mobilité et stimulants économiques*, Nathan, Paris, pp. 59–77.

Chapter 6: 'Real wages and employment – a decade of analysis', Stamp Memorial Lecture, University of London, 1988.

Chapter 7: 'Profitability and factor demands under uncertainty', second Tinbergen Lecture, *De Economist* 137(1) (1989), pp. 2–15.

Introduction

This book may be described both as a tribute to the memory of Professor Federico Caffé and as an outcome of reflections made in the 1980s about the way in which economists could help in the choice of better policies. In Western Europe the main problem to be faced was, of course, unemployment. As a government statistician, an occasional policy adviser and a theorist, I had to pay particular attention to the weakness of the diagnoses on which policies were based. I had then to reflect on the instruments and analytical arguments used at the diagnosis stage.

It was only natural for me to select topics from these reflections when I was asked to lecture, dealing on each occasion with aspects that seemed to deserve the attention of the audience concerned. Some of these lectures were later printed, but often not in widely accessible publications. This book provides an opportunity not only for reproducing the material but also for gathering it in such a way as to make its common purpose more apparent.

Actually the two Caffé Lectures, given at La Sapienza University in Rome, did aim at covering the full range of those recent reflections. They are published here for the first time, respectively as chapters 1 and 4. Three other chapters have appeared so far only in French (2, 3 and 5). Very few libraries are likely to hold both remaining chapters in their stacks at present.

This introduction has two purposes. It aims first at making explicit the common concern and aspiration behind all the chapters, but it is devoted still more to a discussion of what policy advising may be today, after the bitter unemployment experience of the last two decades and after the various attacks upon what was taught in the early 1960s.

1. Economic diagnosis

In medicine a diagnosis consists in identifying an illness after finding and interpreting significant symptoms, for the purpose of curing a patient. Similarly when we speak of economic diagnosis we mean more than forecasting, because (a) we imply one has to search for appropriate signs and for the analytical framework within which they may be interpreted and (b) we suggest that action may be needed. The concept, then, refers both to a wider operation than forecasting and to an operation whose purpose is more focused. The frequency with which the word 'diagnosis' is now being used by economists reveals not only a feeling of urgency because of such problems as unemployment, but also the realization that one cannot rely on a prespecified model of the economy.

The realization explains why so much of this book will not only stress the role of economic analysis but still more discuss what kind of analysis may be appropriate with respect to unemployment. As a background it will be meaningful to recall in this introduction why the confidence in a particular kind of prespecified model was shaken during the past two decades. But the evolution of ideas was so related to the views about policy analysis that it is best described within this context.

Broadly speaking, policy analysis is the function of economists either working for the preparation of government policy or scrutinizing this policy for public debate. Basic to the understanding of the methodological problems, then, is the distribution of roles between politicians and economists. Before we look at this more closely, let us say for now that economists act as experts.

The study of current policies by experts goes through two stages, one for diagnosis about the main characteristics of the situation and of its trends, the other for the determination of the impacts of contemplated measured or even of contemplated policy strategies. The second stage will be considered occasionally here, but is not the main subject. It suffices to note that determination of impacts first requires an understanding of what is happening; more generally, one could not pretend to correct the unsatisfactory features of a situation – be they unemployment, inflation, the trade deficit or still others – if one had no explanation of them. The diagnosis stage has to provide the explanation.

2. Advisers and experts

Issues raised by the distribution of roles between politicians and economists are clearest when one focuses attention on the functions of economic advisers who are employed by governments. It is commonly said that political authorities choose the objectives and priorities, whereas advisers first provide a diagnosis and second study how the various policy instruments ought to be used to attain the objectives most effectively. Advisers would not have to consider the order of priorities. This statement is basically sound in order to provide an ethical reference, but it is so simple that it may give rise to misunderstandings, has disputable implications and was, in fact, disputed.

The statement does not mean that in other contexts economists should refrain from contributing to the enlightenment of the objectives that human societies should aim at achieving. Quite the contrary; philosophers need to know better the economic constraints, the many tradeoffs and their implications with respect to desirable proposals. On some issues of social philosophy the contributions of economists rank among the most valuable. Neither would there be any good ground for preventing economists from entering public debates on the objectives to be assigned to government policies. The only ethical requirement, then, is that they distinguish their role as learned citizens from their role as experts.[1]

Some went so far as to say that, even when acting as experts, economists could not avoid making value judgements (see for instance Klappholz, 1964). One of the most forceful arguments was that the economic language was impregnated with value-loaded connotations suggesting in which direction action ought to go. There is some truth in this argument, particularly when economists profess to contribute to the public debate. But one must also say that, as economic education becomes more widespread, the technical meaning of the words dominates more and more over the emotional connotations. Some obvious ethical rules of behaviour also help to minimize the difficulty.

What remains true, however, is the fact that economists in general and advisers in particular have to interpret the priorities

[1] As often happens with ethical principles, application is not always easy, for instance when economists act as 'partisan advocates' in order to promote their ideas on what ought to be done. This action is the main focus of attention in Nelson (1987).

chosen by public authorities. Quite naturally, these priorities are never stated in directly operational terms. Even when economic language is being used, the statements cannot be precise enough to define an ordering independently of what the constraints may be. In other words, when looking precisely at a particular issue, advisers have to infer the policy choice from general guidelines and from choices made by authorities in other cases.

Such an interpretation requires judgement; one may even say value judgement, it being understood that one then refers to values that derive from the general orientations chosen by the country in its political life. Giersch (1989) brings out this point well when discussing the role of 'public economists' – a wider function than that of just government adviser; for instance: 'When he (or she) sees a problem coming up on the horizon, it is his (her) personal decision and judgement whether it is worth writing about. In raising the issue, one cannot avoid influencing the public's relative valuation of ends that are in conflict with each other' (p. 30). Similarly Wood (1987) recognizes the existence of a dilemma when he writes: 'The adviser represents and bases his advice on "science", that is on technical expertise, while his employer . . . represents action. In practice the interface between these often becomes blurred. If the "scientist" adviser limits his actions to [providing] factual data carrying no value judgements whatsoever, he may be failing in his assigned role of giving pertinent advice. Yet, if he draws too many conclusions from his data he may be usurping the prerogatives of his employer, a process that can lead to the adviser becoming an *éminence grise*.' He also notes: 'The mere fact . . . of [the adviser] being able to express a reasonably unbiased opinion or of coming to conclusions by approaches different from those normally taken by his employer, is in itself an important contribution to the decision-making process of his employer.'

So, economic diagnosis has to find its proper position between two opposing risks. It must avoid providing too little information; in this sense 'A diagnosis combines a positive description and a normative evaluation' (Giersch, 1989, p. 38). But it must also avoid hiding the general values from which this normative evaluation derives, at least if there is any possibility of misunderstanding in this respect.

One should also remember that part of the role of the experts is not directly geared to policy making, but rather to improving the public perception of the problems. In democracies at least, this perception is a fundamental ingredient for the decisions of politicians. This means that experts have to find ways of bringing their results to the attention of the public and have to spend time on this activity. Even an objectively established fact may then have to be made somewhat simpler than it really is, again with a risk of misunderstanding.

3. Policy analysis: historical background

In the 1960s a rather well-defined conception prevailed about what policy analysis was and how it had to proceed. This conception has been repeatedly questioned since then. Ideas are today more varied and often less sure. When dealing with a part of policy analysis, as this book does, an author may now feel obliged to try and explain his or her stance within the range of contemporary conceptions. A way of doing so is for the author broadly to survey the history of the field. I shall distinguish here four parts in this history, with an important overlap between two of them: before Keynes, Keynes (as the best representative of a larger group), the econometricians, and more recent reconsiderations.

Economic advising was already commonplace in the nineteenth century. The case of French economists suffices to show it. Two of them became famous precisely because of their role as policy advisers: Michel Chevalier, trained as an engineer, an adept of the industrialist Saint-Simonian movement, but progressively becoming a proponent of economic liberalism; Courcelle-Seneuil, who now appears as the first good example of a foreign economic expert because of his role in Chile. It seems that in the late nineteenth and early twentieth centuries most economic advisers were hardly more than promoters and guardians of a kind of an orthodoxy concerning the dangers of government interference with so-called economic laws. This may have occurred because of the political pressure for protectionism or because of the political appeal of socialism, both of which were considered as counter-productive by a large majority of the economic profession. This probably had also to do with the state of economic analysis, which provided hardly any other framework for the study of active economic policies than one in which they would be detrimental.[2]

---

[2] Robinson (1983) remarks that in the 1920s 'There was no macro-economics . . . We lived in a world that fluctuated, which we believed to be uncontrollable but somehow self-righting' (p. 260).

Keynes is the most visible and representative figure within the group of deeply involved economists who took a different stand about economic policy matters during the interwar years. His approach was well described by Robinson (1983):

> Faced by [a practical] problem, he tackled it ordinarily in three stages. First, he analysed the problem in all its aspects more searchingly, more radically than any of the rest of us. Second, he set out to discover what factors in the situation had created the problem and what factors needed to be changed if a satisfactory solution was to be achieved . . . Third, and most important, he went ahead to change some institutional setting, to change the traditions of operating some sacrosanct institution, to change the political policies, to change public opinion'. (pp. 256–7)

Remarkable in this quotation is the lack of reference to any 'Keynesian theory'. Each policy problem is said to have been diagnosed and analysed afresh. This is, of course, a simplification. If we look in retrospect at the policy analyses written by Keynes, we may see what his economic theory of the world was, we may compare it with those held by other economists of his generation and we may even find antecedents in the literature. But this theory was not ready-made for applications; it was not his final word; he had to think again about the specifics of each situation.

This probably explains why he was so unsympathetic to the econometricians, and to the work of Jan Tinbergen in particular. What other explanation could there be? Keynes had been influential in the creation of the Central Statistical Office, of British national accounts and of the Economic Section of the Treasury, which was using this empirical base and would later use econometric models. The theory underlying the first generation of econometric models was very much in the spirit of his own ideas. To outside observers Keynes and the econometricians could only appear as close cousins. But one may guess Keynes did not want his approach to new problems and his intuition about their proper analysis to be constrained by the straitjacket of a preconceived econometric model.

4. The 1960 methodology

Econometricians in the 1940s were indeed well engaged in founding, for policy analysis, a methodology that was to become the main reference twenty years later. The Dutch school following Jan Tinbergen and the Norwegian school inspired by Ragnar Frisch were born; Lawrence Klein was becoming ready to promote the methodology in the United States and throughout the world.

The principle was to analyse the effects of contemplated policies within a macroeconometric model that would be the best available representation of the dynamics underlying economic evolution. The model would give the best prediction of the effects, so that the choice of policies would be based on objective and sound assessment of feasibilities and tradeoffs. The principle was based on two propositions: (i) policy analysis requires forecasts, (ii) macroeconometric models provide the best forecasting tool. The two following quotations are interesting to read again today.

> *Gouverner c'est prévoir* is perhaps an exaggeration – it means [not only that policy-making] requires prediction . . . but that there is an identity . . . between both concepts; . . . however, prediction plays such an essential role in the policy-making process that this French dictum may be accepted as a vivid expression of an important requirement for rational policy. Rational policy-making is the adaptation of the policy-maker's instruments to his changing environment in such a way that the result is 'good' or even 'optimal' . . . First, the changing environment has to be predicted; second, a forecast of the effects of the policy-maker's measures, i.e. of changes of instrument values, is required; third, a plan of action must be made. (Theil, 1958, pp. 2–3)

> We want . . . to discover the best possible theory or theories which explain the fluctuations we observe. If we know the quantitative characteristics of the economic system, we shall be able to forecast . . . the course of certain economic magnitudes such as employment, output, or income; and we shall also be able to forecast . . . the effect upon the system of various economic policies . . . We view the economic system as describable by a set of simultaneous equations expressing all the interrelationships among the measurable economic magnitudes which guide economic behavior. (Klein, 1950, pp. 1–2)

The point of departure between Keynes and the econometricians was proposition (ii) above, or equivalently Klein's last sentence. It is, indeed, where one may dispute the methodology that was widely adopted in the 1960s. But clarity of the discussion requires that one distinguishes between the several methodological choices that were made with confidence when experts decided to rely on forecasting from macroeconometric models. I think it is appropriate to list six such choices:

(i) Proper forecasts cannot be just 'judgemental'.
(ii) Proper forecasts cannot come just from statistical extrapolation.
(iii) Proper forecasts cannot come just from pure economic reasoning with no reference to statistical data except for a rough description of the current situation.
(iv) Proper forecasts cannot come from partial models neglecting feedback resulting from important macroeconomic relationships.
(v) Proper forecasts can come from a macroeconometric model built before the specifics of the current situation were known.
(vi) Proper forecasts can come from the type of macroeconometric models that were experimented with by, for instance, Lawrence Klein.

My purpose here is not to discuss where in this list Keynes disagreed with the econometricians; I have already suggested he could not accept (v); I have reasons to think he would have frowned upon (iii). But this is secondary today, when we want to assess the value of the criticism raised much more recently against the methodology promoted by econometricians.

Before turning to this criticism I must, however, pause at choice (i), which was not explicitly criticized but with respect to which mental reservations remain, especially when one speaks about the role of diagnosis in policy analysis. By 'judgemental forecast' can only be meant one that is left to the judgement of the expert. But a forecast ought not to be accepted blindly. Having good judgement does not discharge the expert from the duty of explaining how the conclusion was reached; then the expert will reveal having made methodological choices covered by points (ii) to (vi), even if not formalizing the procedure. It goes without saying that, whatever the methodology, judgement is required to apply it well in each case.

5. New assessments

I need not dwell on the fact that the macroeconometric methodology is no longer presented in academic teaching with the same confidence as it was thirty years ago. Even such a good representative of the Norwegian school as Leif Johansen was careful in the following statement given shortly before his death:

> Considered as a trend the development in the direction of more widespread use of econometric models will hardly be reversed. However, the trend is not quite stable and invulnerable. Lack of success, conspicuous failures, and inability to come to grips with important problems because of inadequate formulations may drive the models more or less off the scene; political developments in the direction of more modest and less detailed targets for economic policy, or more reliance on free market mechanisms and simple rules for economic policy may also reduce the need for econometric models in connection with policy-making. (Johansen, 1982, pp. 91–2)

Indeed, one first notes that quite a few economists advocate a return to the concept of policy advising that prevailed at the beginning of the century. Such was for long the position taken by Milton Friedman, who argued repeatedly against government attempts at stabilizing business fluctuations. Ideas put forward by some adepts of the public choice movement go in the same direction. Even more specific and technical critiques on the econometric methodology often lead their authors to suggest that active macroeconomic strategies are bound to fail. Policy advising would then not need precise forecasts, or rather the type of useful forecasts would be given by pure economic reasoning, in contradiction to principle (iii) above.

The revival of this position imposes a serious reflection to those dissenting from it. In the first Caffé Lecture, published here as chapter 1, I present in simple terms some of my arguments why macroeconomic public control of modern market economies is needed. I have written enough elsewhere for a long explanation to be superfluous here (in particular Malinvaud, 1984 and 1991a). My position of course draws on what I believe to be satisfactory theories about the functioning of these economies.

A quite valuable point was, however, made by the critics of the practice used in the 1960s, namely that policy analysis then neglected important feedback generated by the budgetary or monetary measures that were discussed. Some of this feedback in particular comes from the fact that a government decision reveals something about the way in which policy-makers react to changes in their environment. While the expert tends to think about the decision as if it were an isolated act with no implication for future actions, economic agents may interpret it as a sign of what the government strategy really is and will be. Such an interpretation may lead to private behaviour quite different from that assumed by the expert. In other words, when forecasting the effects of government measures, one should be clear about what is really at stake: major political decisions in the economic field may concern the 'policy regime' more than the particular budget discussed or the interest rate at a particular time. This makes policy analysis more difficult, but does not in itself fundamentally change the methodology; indeed it amounts to taking principle (iv) still more seriously into account than was earlier found to be necessary.

What was called New Classical Macroeconomics rejected, above all, assertion (vi) and claimed that the current macroeconometric models were not theoretically sound: their rationalization of behaviour was incomplete; their representation of markets was inadequate. The criticism was more than the normal expression of the feeling that better specifications would improve the reliability of macroeconometric models. It amounted to saying that a completely new paradigm had to be used for macroeconomic thinking: the hypothesis of rational behaviour had to be made more systematic and to contain in particular what was called rational expectations; all markets had to be viewed as exactly and permanently cleared. Such a stance forces anyone to take sides: to be for New Classical Macroeconomics and then to reject the earlier methodology, or to believe that the principle of this earlier methodology remains appropriate and to reject New Classical Macroeconomics. Being faced with such a dichotomy I believe that the 1960 line of attack on policy analysis still is the proper one, notwithstanding some theoretical progress due to research done under the auspices of New Classical Macroeconomics.

Indeed, what alternative was proposed? During some years it was the creed of 'policy ineffectiveness', a phrase which was claimed to be proved true by arguments applied to outrageously simple models of the economic system. This creed recommended 'laissez-faire' and amounted to a return to the conception of policy advising that was current at the beginning of the century.

Now the so-called Real Business Cycles school proposes the study of macroeconomic models, which are claimed to be based on a deeper analysis than those used by econometricians; these models contain parameters that are related to the fundamental determinants of behaviour (and for this reason named 'deep parameters'). I shall not discuss here for lack of space the 'calibration' that aims at giving realistic numerical values to the parameters. The main point is to note that the class of such models is potentially suited for policy analysis, by the same kind of procedures as are applied with current macroeconometric models. The question then is to know whether the new models so obtained are more reliable than the older ones.

A 'final' answer to the question may be premature because these new models are still evolving, and in the direction of making them closer to those used by macroeconometricians. But the first generation of these models presented such a distorted representation of phenomena that it was clearly unsuited, for instance, for analysis of any policy package intended to stimulate the demand for labour in order to reduce unemployment. Moreover, I am inclined to believe that the models in question will never be fully corrected for their original sin: to be rooted not in the full range of available observations about the economic system, but in the application to short and medium-run macroeconomics of a theory built for other purposes.

Another alternative to the 1960 methodology stands at the opposite extreme from the ones discussed so far. In contradiction to statement (ii) on p. 8 it wants to use only macroeconomic time series for forecasting economic evolution and even for analysing policies (Doan et al., 1984). This alternative, whose main advocate was Christopher Sims, is briefly presented here in chapters 2 and 3, where it is related to a fundamental debate about the application of econometric inference in macroeconomics. Since its recommendations for policy analysis do not now seem likely to be followed in practice, I shall not comment more about it in this introduction.

At the end of this discussion my own position should already be fairly clear. Let me add, however, that I do not wish to appear dogmatic. Indeed, I am often hesitant in choosing what to say about the most appropriate way of dealing with issues related to what is considered here. Concerning, for instance, the reliability of the macroeconometric models used during the past decades I am sure improvements are feasible, even for those conditional projections for which these models are best suited: macroeconomic evolutions at the horizon of one to three years. For shorter horizons the main macroeconomic evolutions are equally well forecast by pure statistical extrapolation and the effects of such policy decisions as a rise in the central bank interest rate can properly be found by partial analysis (notwithstanding statements (ii) and (iv) at the end of section 4). For longer horizons my doubts will appear here in the chapters concerning unemployment. Even for the intermediate favourable range, the impacts of some uncommon policy decisions motivated by particular concerns may not be properly estimated by existing models and a purely theoretical reasoning, preferably confirmed by historical references, may provide a better evaluation (statements (iii) and (v) notwithstanding).

I am sure my position is widely shared, except for secondary shades of opinions, by those directly or indirectly involved in policy advising. Undogmatic reliance on macroeconometric projections characterizes what is done in national and international administrations, for instance at the OECD as described in chapter 3. But the frequent use of the word 'diagnosis' instead of 'forecast' also means that symptoms have to be sought; it suggests that they may not always appear through the set of conditional forecasts produced by a macroeconometric model built before the specifics of the current situation were known.

It is, then, fair to say that the dominant attitude among those actually involved in policy analysis differs somewhat from the one inspiring those who, like Jan Tinbergen, wrote on the theory of economic policy forty years ago. The literature of that time stressed immediate forecasts and the role of the model that would produce them. The word diagnosis was seldom used, if at all.

6. The challenge of high unemployment

In Western Europe at least, high unemployment was and unfortunately still is the main problem challenging economic diagnosis.[3] This was also the problem that most disturbed Federico Caffé in the last part of his life. Each of these two reasons would make the challenge worthy of special scrutiny in this book. But I must avoid as far as possible repeating ideas already presented elsewhere (particularly in Malinvaud, 1984). At this stage I shall limit myself to a brief introduction to the last four chapters of the book.

[3] Mass unemployment is also a challenge for economic theory. But it is a quite different challenge that is not discussed in this book. On the distinction between the two challenges see Malinvaud (1990) particularly pp. 23–4.

There is a challenge because professional economists did not reach, during this long period, sufficient consensus about the diagnosis of the phenomenon. There is some degree of consensus among economists and, to this extent, the diagnosis was largely accepted by public opinion. Almost everybody agrees that high unemployment means an excess supply of labour and is due to a deficiency of the demand for labour. Almost everybody agrees on the proximate causes of this deficiency: the disorder of the world economy since 1971, the increasing competition from Japan and the Newly Industrialized Countries, and finally a particularly poor European adaptation to the new situation that was so created. But this consensus did not suffice for the identification of symptoms suggesting how the problem could have been cured: in what way and for what reason was European adaptation poor? Here ideas diverged to a greater or lesser degree depending on the policy issue that was at stake; they diverged for instance about the role of wage rates, which is discussed in chapter 6.

The force of the challenge appears if I refer here to the very interesting book of the Brookings Institution, edited by Lawrence and Schultze (1987), who wanted to explain why European growth had been so slow since the middle of the 1970s. The book deserves attention because it applies to carefully observed facts the positive and rigorous approach to which there is no reliable alternative for diagnosing macroeconomic problems. I can only agree on two general conclusions proposed by the editors. First, a slowing down of European growth had to occur after the outstanding but unsustainable performance of the previous decades during which European output caught up with its long-run increasing potential, but a more gentle slowing down was conceivable and would have maintained full employment. Second, any monolithic explanation of the disappointing stagnation of the period 1973–83 would be erroneous: neither the weakening of economic incentives induced in particular by the welfare state, nor the disequilibrium in the structure of prices and remuneration rates, nor economic policy mistakes in demand management after the oil shocks could, taken alone, provide a satisfactory explanation; one has to take all these factors into account simultaneously, while also explaining each of them. But the diagnosis must be specific enough to be useful. It must identify those parts of the phenomena which played particularly strategic roles.

At this last stage Lawrence and Schultze conclude that the main structural sources of European problems were concentrated in the labour markets. *A contrario* they find no serious problem with the markets for goods and in particular with a conceivable deterioration of European competitiveness. This conclusion is disputable and deserves particular attention. Of course, the allocation of responsibilities between markets for labour and markets for goods depends on what is meant by it; it depends on the conceptual framework used for integrating within an overall system the results of many detailed analysis and for thinking about possible cures. This is where theoretical knowledge comes into its own.

A frequent practice, which is also sometimes used in the book, assumes a conceptual framework that I find to be particularly inappropriate in the search for causes of unemployment. I may somewhat caricature it the better to show its presuppositions. The central concept is the famous NAIRU: the non-accelerating inflation rate of unemployment. This rate is computed from fits of a price equation and of the modern Phillips Law according to which variations in the growth rate of nominal wages are explained by variations in (i) the expected growth rate of prices and (ii) the unemployment rate. The concept of a NAIRU is not necessarily bad and I admit it may be used in explanatory studies of inflation and in inflation diagnosis. But many macroeconomists nowadays also give a central role to the NAIRU in their explanation of unemployment. This practice assumes that, in order to explain variations in unemployment, it would be enough to explain shifts in the price equation and in the Phillips curve; inverting the causal relation underlying the price–wage block would suffice. Indeed, one finds cases in which, after a close examination of the inflationary process, the macroeconomist discussing unemployment does not even mention the labour supply or the demand for labour.

I have two objections against this practice. First, I believe there is much more stability in the laws of the labour supply and of the demand for labour than in the macroeconomic laws describing the process of inflation. Second, studying the labour supply and the demand for labour is a more direct and more transparent approach to the explanation of unemployment than concentrating on the study of inflation; we are too little advanced in our macroeconomic knowledge for neglecting direct explanations and going straight to indirect ones.

7. The demand for labour

A second methodological critique of mine to current practice in attempting to explain unemployment has to do with what I believe to be important clues for the explanation. My critique concerns the appropriate concept of the demand for labour and the corresponding articulation between the market for labour and the market for goods. In order to be clear in what follows, I may first indicate where I see clues (i.e. symptoms).

It seems to me that the results of past research lead us to two important conclusions. First, the main responsibility in the disappointing evolution of the demand for labour belongs to autonomous factors that acted on the demand for goods: mostly because of the problems of the world economy, somewhat also because of European macroeconomic policies. Second, the evolution of real remuneration rates played a perverse role: the bulge of real wage rates in the 1970s led to an important distortion of the relative cost of labour with respect to capital, hence to a too strong substitution of capital for labour; it also damaged profit rates, which were further depressed in the 1980s by the high level of real interest rates; this depression stopped the increase of productive capacities up to 1985, thus damaging for years European non-price competitiveness.

In order to capture these important trends, analysis of the demand for labour must stress medium-term determinants. But the common approach has been to accept a short-term vision of this demand and to study it as resulting, each year, from an exogenous production function confronted with current economic conditions concerning in particular wage and interest rates. Such a vision leads one to think as if shifts in the production function were also exogenous, hence to miss the most important link between remuneration rates and the demand for labour, namely the one concerning the determinants of the volume and nature of investment.

This need for a change of analysis is argued carefully in chapter 6. If accepted, it implies that, in order to understand the demand for labour, understanding the demand for capital by firms is also required. This brings into scope another issue, whose difficulty is well recognized: investment reflects the strategy of firms placed in an evolving economic and financial environment, where information is never complete; choices then are to a large extent irreversible, even when major decisions are delayed. But this extra complication is not artificial; recruitments and disbandings are part of firms' strategy on a par with investments.

In my reflection on employment I have chosen a particular model of the demand for capital. This model is the subject of chapter 7; its results are used in chapter 6 and in several of my other writings. A representative firm is faced with uncertainty as to future demand for its output; it knows the cost of capital; it has expectations concerning the wage rate; it must select in advance both a productive capacity and an input mix. I believe this model captures the features that most matter for analysing the impact of remuneration rates on the medium-term evolution of the demand for labour. But I am aware that it also misses other features that may at times become important, for instance financial constraints. I claim little more for this model than its contribution to showing how a method for medium-term analysis of the demand for labour can be put to work.

Articulation of the market for goods with the market for labour is an important aspect of any conceptual framework for employment diagnosis, as was pointed out in section 6 above. The articulations identified in my own framework appear in the last section of chapter 4. They are made still more explicit in another of my articles, which is not reproduced here (Malinvaud, 1991b).

8. Frictional and disequilibrium unemployment

Most economists agree that mass unemployment in Western Europe should be first and foremost recognized as being an excess supply of labour. This is why in the preceding two sections I focused attention on this disequilibrium. But unemployment diagnosis has also to consider symptoms that would not be related to changes in the true excess supply on the labour market. These symptoms could concern changes in the speed of turnover of the labour force from one job to another with an interim period of unemployment, or changes in the average time spent unemployed by those people who eventually give up searching for a job and so leave the labour force. They could concern changes in the match between the structures of the labour supply and of the demand for labour, by qualification, localization and the like. Such changes concern a part of measured unemployment that does not correspond to an excess supply of labour. It is customary to call this part 'frictional unemployment'.

But the concept of frictional unemployment is delicate. Its definition requires the simultaneous definition of other concepts occurring in a precise description of the labour market and its operation. Moreover, if it is to be applied numerically, the definition requires conventions about where precisely to draw the line separating the two components of unemployment. This is discussed at some length at the beginning of chapter 4.

It will become apparent that separation between unemployment and excess supply of labour refers to the observation of the number of vacant jobs as well as to the number of unemployed workers. Indeed, one may show that, for any given level of the rate of frictional unemployment, a relation holds between the vacancy rate and the unemployment rate, as currently measured. Conversely, observing these two last rates permits us to infer what the first one is. The relation that so identifies frictional unemployment is now called 'the Beveridge curve'. Definition of this curve and analysis of the determinants of its shifts thus become important indirect ingredients of unemployment diagnosis. Chapter 5 is devoted to this subject, about which the economic literature does not seem to be fully satisfactory at present.

This book raises a number of questions without giving even a provisional answer to many of them. Thus, much remains to be done, even within the limited domain discussed here. Of this simple truth Federico Caffè was well aware. Like Keynes when confronted with an actual issue 'he analysed the problem in all its aspects more searchingly, more radically' than most others would have done. Such an attitude will long have to be recommended, considering how complex are the phenomena with which we economists have to deal.

References

T. Doan, R. Litterman and C. Sims (1984), 'Forecasting and conditional projections using realistic prior distributions', *Econometric Reviews*, 3(1), pp. 1–100.

H. Giersch (1989), 'On being a public economist', in Herbert Giersch (ed.), *Paolo Baffi International Prize for Economics*, San Paolo, Turin.

L. Johansen (1982), 'Econometric models and economic planning and policy', in M. Hazelwinkel and A. Rinnoy Kan (eds.), *Current Developments in the Interface: Economics, Econometrics, Mathematics*, Reidel, Dordrecht, pp. 91–120.

K. Klappholz (1964), 'Value judgments and economics', *British Journal for the Philosophy of Science*, 15, pp. 95–114, reprinted in D. Hausman (ed.), *The Philosophy of Economics – An Anthology*, Cambridge University Press, Cambridge, 1984, pp. 276–92.

L. Klein (1950), *Economic Fluctuations in the United States, 1921–1941*, Wiley, New York.

R. Lawrence and C. Schultze (1987) (eds.), *Barriers to European Growth: A Transatlantic View*, The Brookings Institution, Washington.

E. Malinvaud (1984), *Mass Unemployment*, Basil Blackwell, Oxford.

(1990), 'What do we mean by explaining high unemployment?', *Structural Change and Economic Dynamics*, 1(1), pp. 15–26.

(1991a), 'Incomplete market clearing', in L. McKenzie and S. Zamagni (eds.), *Value and Capital – Fifty Years Later*, Macmillan, London, pp. 179–96.

(1991b), 'A medium-term employment equilibrium', in W. Barnett, B. Cornet, C. d'Aspremont, J. Gabszewicz and A. Mas-Colell (eds.), *Equilibrium Theory and Applications*, Cambridge University Press, Cambridge, pp. 319–37.

R. Nelson (1987), 'The economics profession and the making of public policy', *Journal of Economic Literature*, 25, pp. 49–91.

A. Robinson (1983), 'Impressions of Maynard Keynes', in D. Worswick and J. Trevithick (eds.), *Keynes and the Modern World*, Cambridge University Press, Cambridge, pp. 255–61.

H. Theil (1958), *Economic Forecasts and Policy*, North Holland, Amsterdam.

J. Wood (1987), 'Advisers' in J. Eatwell, M. Milgate and P. Newman (eds.), *The New Palgrave*, Macmillan, London.

1

Expert diagnosis

Good diagnosis requires good observations and the existence of good explanatory theories. Improving on observations and theories are the means by which one can really reach improvement in diagnosis. But for this progress to be most effective with respect to the needs of policy analysis, priorities must be identified correctly. They of course depend on the ultimate aims of the analysis, which ought never to be forgotten. They also depend on the type of situation one is facing; indeed, the economy does not function like a linear system in which the main endogenous variables exhibit constant degrees of sensitivity with respect to policy instruments – such a conception often provides a sufficient approximation for small variations with respect to the current situation, but the linear approximation then depends on what this situation really is. An important aspect of the diagnosis consists in so identifying the determinants to which the economy will particularly react at the time of study.

In the first part of this lecture I shall briefly outline the purposes assigned to macroeconomic diagnosis in our economies. The second part will be devoted to observations, not so much to the collection of data as to their first analysis. The third part will concern the theoretical framework or frameworks to be used in our explanations.

1. The purpose of diagnosis in market economies

The ideal vision of free market economies operating with perfect efficiency provides, in our case as in many others, the best starting point because it is the only well-articulated and well-understood

First Caffè Lecture 1990.

19

reference at our disposal. The models supporting this vision are certainly abstract and neglect important features of the real world, but they take full account of other important aspects, particularly of the existence of markets and of a price system ruling most kinds of economic behaviour. With the background of these models, we can think about the functions given to expert diagnosis in our economies.

   (i) We know that one major difficulty faced by any kind of economic organization is to take proper account of all the relevant information that exists for an efficient use of resources. In market economies agents are given almost complete freedom in the use of the information they have about the present and future conditions of their own activities and about their immediate environment; the prices convey to them a measure of current relative scarcities of goods and services, although often an imperfect measure; but agents also need more relevant global information for detecting the future trends of the economy in which they are living.[1] The diagnosis of experts provides this kind of information to them.

This first function may be fulfilled privately, either in very large corporations by specially appointed experts, or else by consulting firms that sell their diagnosis to users and may then consider the questions concerning more particularly their clients. Most often, however, the diffusion of information about the current situation and its future trends is provided as a public service to all those interested. The producers of this service either are the same experts as those who advise on policy, or they are people working with the same methodology, often in close connection with the former. This important role of the diagnosis work must not be overlooked.

It implies one main additional consideration beyond those required for the preparation of economic policies, namely that firms and households would like to have the kind of information that

---

[1] It was sometimes argued that the price system is able to provide this kind of information also. But even neglecting the difficulties in the proof of properties supporting this idea in the theory of the general competitive equilibrium with complete markets and no search cost, it would be quite unrealistic to recognize any relevance to the idea in the context of our present discussion (Jordan and Radner, 1982; Grossman and Stiglitz, 1980).

would be provided by proper markets if they existed. They would like to know how the prices of the goods and services they will have to buy will evolve not only in the immediate future but over the period that matters for their decisions, a horizon that often extends over more than a decade. Clearly expert diagnosis dealing with macroeconomic evolution cannot go very far in satisfying this demand; but it should at least try to detect what might be the medium-term trend in real wage rates and real interest rates.

(ii) For contributing to the preparation of economic policies, diagnosis should concern the various aspects calling for policy intervention, precisely because free operation of markets cannot be relied on from these viewpoints. I shall not consider here industrial or trade policies and the regulation of competition, because they would take us too far away from the macroeconomic field to which my subject belongs – the experts of which I am speaking do indeed work within this field. For the preparation of industrial or similar policies there is also a diagnostic phase to which many of my comments would apply; but it is the work of somewhat different experts.

Policy makers are concerned by the lack of equity in some market evolutions. Macroeconomic indicators provide a good deal of the required characterization in this respect. For instance a reversal of the trend that had previously pushed toward more equal income distributions occurred in Western Europe at the beginning of the 1980s; this reversal is well traced to the rise in real interest rates, to an increased wage flexibility intended to reactivate labour incentives, to the restoration of profit margins that had been too far depressed and to the decrease in the effective tax rate on capital incomes. Most of these shifts are observable in macroeconomic statistics. Our people now realize that the tradeoff between equity and employment is more severe than they had earlier thought; hence they understand the recent increase in inequalities; but they are not ready to forsake the central European social philosophy, which moved Federico Caffé among many others and values equity highly. This means that experts have to say whether the trend of the past years will go on, or come to a pause.

Policy makers are still more concerned about two important kinds of unsatisfactory trends in short-term evolution. Inflation is a depreciation of nominally denominated assets and of the currency used as the unit in economic transactions; inflation is rightly felt to be a failure of authorities in charge of guaranteeing the value of money; political powers have the duty to counteract this evolution, particularly when the rate of inflation accelerates. Unemployment, as soon as it concerns a sizable proportion of the labour force, appears as a social evil, which obviously ought to be eradicated. Inflation and unemployment result from an imperfect functioning of a price system which does not fulfil its allocative function; one may speak of them as showing the existence of unwanted disequilibria.

Other characteristics of short-run evolution may also appear as unsustainable for long and as therefore requiring early correction induced by policy intervention. This may be the case of a sizable deficit of the balance of payments or of an increasing trend in an already heavy government debt. In both cases one anticipates that the longer the disequilibrium persists, the more painful will the correction have to be. Present political authorities hence have an obvious duty to at least alleviate deficits.

Since we all understand the usefulness of a good diagnosis about these short-term disequilibria, inflation, unemployment, increase in national or government debt, I need not elaborate on them at this stage. But attention ought not to be limited to them. The experience of the last two decades has, on the contrary, led us to realize that economic policy has more to do than just to bring short-term corrections to unwanted trends. It has more to do because corrections so conceived may at times worsen the situation to be faced later or may even at times be downright impossible to make. Economic policy, then, has also to take a longer-term viewpoint, to be concerned with all the main requirements of economic growth, in particular with the competitiveness of the economy. Experts have therefore also to diagnose the difficulties of the next decade, as well as the opportunities it can offer. In other words, depending on what public decisions are, the market system can stimulate more or less competitiveness, growth, employment and increases in levels of living; the best conditions in this respect may not be easy to find, but neither can they be claimed to follow directly from such a simple rule as 'laisser faire', whatever exactly it might mean in practice. Dealing correctly with these longer-term prospects is particularly challenging for expert diagnosis.

2. Observation

(i) Good diagnosis requires good observation, hence, before anything else, accurate collection of statistical data. Since dealing adequately with this first requirement would take us too far out of our main subject, I shall just make here one, more particularly topical, comment about it.[2]

The statistical basis of macroeconomics has been much developed in most countries for over forty years, notably in order to provide the tools needed for determining the stance of Keynesian policies. In their effort to improve on the quality of the information provided, statisticians must choose priorities since the human and financial resources of official agencies are limited while good statistics are costly. The choice of these priorities raises dilemmas, in particular as between aiming at reducing inaccuracies of existing statistics and at providing new statistics on aspects not covered so far. Statisticians, well aware of existing inaccuracies, often tend to choose the first objective while some users regret that the second is not chosen.

A particular application of this general remark concerns national accounts and the macroeconomic data on which they are based: whereas the flow or income accounts are regularly presented, the stock or wealth accounts are rare and the progress in producing them is very slow. But the broadening of the concerns of economic policies, toward the supply side of the economy and toward longer-term problems, also means that the diagnosis must bear on stocks of productive capital and private wealth as well as on the more commonly available flows that aggregate demand analysis has been used to consider. Macroeconomists should, I believe, insist on the importance of regular data on stocks, even at the cost of some of the flow data provided now. I know that the proposal is more easily made than applied; but it is up to macroeconomists to express their priorities clearly.

(ii) Collection, processing and diffusion of data by official statisticians does not suffice for experts in charge of diagnosis to embark directly on the search for

---

[2] The importance for diagnosis of data collection is *de facto* acknowledged when the task of making projections is given to statisticians, a quite common case. On this contribution of statisticians see chapter 3 in this book.

explanations. Analysts of business conditions have long known that they must still scrutinize the data in order to detect the most relevant trends that are present in them; indeed, these trends are not immediately apparent. In other words experts must still process the available data, taking into account the particular concerns that motivate their search for a diagnosis. This processing belongs to the realm of statistical data analysis when it is intended to isolate and characterize particular components of time series; it belongs to the realm of economic analysis when it aims at computing particular indicators on specific aspects of the phenomena under consideration. Let us look briefly in turn at each of these two types of processing.

The traditional decomposition of time series distinguishes four components: the random short-term fluctuation, the seasonal component, the long-term trend and the remaining component, often loosely called 'the cycle'. The statistical techniques for the decomposition have been closely studied for many years, both in mathematical statistics, for the determination of efficient techniques, and in economic statistics, for meeting the needs of business and government analysts. A perfect solution will never be found since the desirable requirements somewhat conflict with one another. But the professional practice is sure enough to allow competent diagnosis.

One aspect of this practice has, however, been recently reconsidered and directly concerns our subject. It bears on our concept of medium or long-term trend. The traditional decomposition implicitly assumed that the trend had to be dealt with as deterministic and shorter-term fluctuations as random. The intuition behind such a way of dealing with the data was probably often that the series commonly used were too short to lend themselves to the discovery of any low-frequency random component.

But the practice had a consequence for predictive diagnosis; it led to the recommendation that the trend be simply extrapolated with the functional form given to it in the data analysis: for instance if the trend had been fitted by an exponential function of time, the long-term evolution was forecast to be along this same exponential. When a mathematical model was chosen in order to represent the generation of the series, the assumption of a deterministic trend of a particular functional form was usually made explicit, the random component of the series being specified as a realization of a stationary process with a zero mean. This implied that, as the forecast was supposed to be extended to longer and longer horizons, the estimated variance of the forecasting error quickly came close to a finite limit: in practice the forecast up to ten years did not seem to be notably more uncertain than the forecast up to three years. This kind of representation has recently been questioned, and rightly so; but the alternative proposed by some economists is also too extreme to be fully convincing.

The opposite extreme to a deterministic trend is a random walk; this is a process with which the natural forecast for all future dates is the last observed value, the variance of the forecasting error then being proportional to the distance up to the date of forecast. For some economic data observed at high frequency a random walk gives a good approximation; this is the case for daily quotations on the stock exchange, including quotations of exchange rates and of bond prices.[3] Some economists have argued in favour of modelling many economic series as random walks (see for instance Nelson and Plosser, 1982). What conclusion follows for our subject, which concerns macroeconomic diagnosis?

We should recognize that some erratic changes have much more permanence than was traditionally assumed. Hence, random walk components may be appropriate for modelling these erratic changes; but this does not imply a complete revision of our present practice, because the random walk hypothesis may appear as too extreme and because analysis of changes in deterministic components will remain important for our diagnosis.

The random walk hypothesis appears as too extreme even for the forecast of such variables as real exchange rates and real interest rates in macroeconomic analysis. The horizon then is usually much longer than the weeks, months or even quarters for which a random walk process would appear as satisfactory (remember by the way that official macroeconomic forecasts most often make the 'conventional' hypothesis of unchanged exchange rates). Over the horizon

---

[3] Actually a better approximation for financial series takes into account the observed fact that changes occur in the variance of erratic movements, this variance being at times high for a more or less-long period, at other times low. But this complication has secondary importance for our present discussion.

of a few years or more a 'reversal to the mean' may be observed; this means a tendency for the evolution to come back to some normal level, which, for instance for real exchange rates, may be considered as given by purchasing power parities. In other words the random process that would correctly represent the evolution would not be quite a random walk; a better approximation would be offered by, say, a first-order autoregressive process with an autocorrelation coefficient that would be quite close to one, but slightly lower. For many applications the difference does not matter much and a random walk is a better assumption than an auto-regressive process with only a moderate autocorrelation; but for other applications the independent study of the normal level and of its possible deterministic evolution becomes important.

For major trends, such as those of global factor productivity, a deterministic component is unavoidable since the series obviously tends to increase. This is recognized by advocates of the random walk hypothesis, who then introduce a 'random walk with drift', the drift being deterministic. But the importance of a careful study of this deterministic component and of the changes that it may have undergone is not always stressed, as it should be. In other words, even admitting that some future shocks to productivity with per-manent effects may be unpredictable, one needs to scrutinize care-fully whether past evolution shows a tendency toward acceleration, retardation, or any other sustained change in evolution. Identifying such changes obviously helps in making a better diagnosis.

(iii) Let us now turn our attention to a kind of data analysis that is still more directly motivated by the conceptualization of economic phenomena. Official macroeconomic statistics must often be supplemented by specific indicators that researchers have to compute themselves from data of varying accessibility. I shall just give here an idea of the existence and diversity of such useful indicators that are not yet recognized by those in charge of the standard production and diffusion of economic data, and in some cases not even recognized in the teaching of economics.

The notion of the *full employment budget* no longer seems to be as fashionable as it was at the time of great confidence in Keynesian economics. I believe it is still significant. But defining it requires a definition of full employment, hence a decomposition of unemployment into a frictional part and a part measuring the excess supply of labour. This decomposition is more generally useful in all kinds of macroeconomic diagnoses on employment. I shall come back to it in the subsequent chapters.

For diagnosis about the real stance of fiscal policy, about the trend in profit rates or about many other features of macroeconomic evolution one must often try to correct national account figures for the *effects of inflation*, which induces regular and anticipated real capital gains or losses that ought to be treated as positive or negative incomes.

Some of the recently developed quantitative tools are intended to characterize less aggregated and more structural features of the economy. For example, an extensive literature has appeared on the measurement of the *cost of capital*, often depending on its mode of financing, and on effective rates of taxation. Similarly *effective rates of protection and subsidy* have been computed for the analysis of international trade (Balassa et al., 1971; 1982).

The various quantitative tools mentioned above, and others as well, have in common the fact that they may be viewed as intermediate products. They are the result of more or less elaborate processing of available data from standard collections of macroeconomic statistics or from microeconomic sources of information. In turn they are intended to serve in the analysis of other questions; they are more interesting as input for this analysis than as end products.

The rationale for the existence and importance of this production of intermediate indicators lies in the exploratory nature of some of our investigations, even when we want to assess the impact of alternative policies. In many areas of macroeconomics, research does not operate within the confines of a completely given theoretical model. While the general concern of the research is usually clear, even the precise questions to be answered may not be formulated until after a first examination of the reality at issue. Measurement of precisely defined, even if unfamiliar, concepts appears to be a necessary first step for a fruitful exploration.

Progress in the methods for producing such intermediate quantitative tools is the responsibility of those working in the various fields in which these tools are used. But the definition, calculation and discussion of these intermediate indicators also play an important role in promoting efficiency of the whole chain from observation to diagnosis and inference. Pausing at an intermediate stage enables us to spot, more clearly than otherwise, the deficiencies in accuracy or relevance of the available statistical material; so experts can provide useful feedback to statisticians who may, as a result, bring improvements to their collection and processing of data. In addition, the conceptual work done at the intermediate level must take into account real features that theory tends to neglect; it may thus stimulate reexamination of the theory and possibly a reformulation that will make it more satisfactory.

3. Theoretical framework

A clear sign of the maturity of economics lies in the existence of a system of well specified concepts, most of which are measurable, or even regularly measured. This system is progressively becoming more rich, as new concepts are being invented or made more precise. A case in point is the one I just discussed, namely the use and diffusion of still unconventional indicators intended to give a better grasp on various aspects of economic structures and evolution.

Since concepts are always related to particular ways of looking at the world, one has often pointed out that they were 'theory impregnated'. But the so-called theory underlying the use of a concept may be quite rudimentary. Indeed, for the most familiar concepts the theory is so rudimentary that everyone takes it for granted. For instance when we speak of the price level we have in mind the purchasing power of a given sum of money and we assume that a person holding this sum will be free to use it for buying the goods he or she wants; we also assume that the price system works in such a way as to impose a fairly common pattern to the simultaneous changes of all prices, so that different people will usually experience similar changes in the purchasing power of the same quantity of money even though they are not buying the same goods. When we build an index of the price level, we have to make the theoretical reference more precise; it is well known that this reference is then never perfectly satisfactory, whether it is purely statistical or also rooted in the microeconomic theory of prices; but the concept and its measure are so useful that we accept the imperfection, which amounts to saying that we rely on the type of rudimentary theory mentioned above.

In itself the existence of a rich system of commonly accepted concepts does not then prove much about the degree of theoretical development and theoretical unity of a discipline. This is why we must look more carefully into the question. What kind of theoretical framework or frameworks do macroeconomists use for their diagnoses, or could they use? In answer to this question, I shall try to argue that there is indeed a basic common theoretical framework within which all kinds of macroeconomic explanations are being posed and discussed. But this framework remains fairly general and does not suffice for the determination of a diagnosis. Different groups of theories then serve for the main kinds of issues that experts have to examine.

(i) The common theoretical notion is to view economic evolution as being made of a sequence of temporary equilibria, each equilibrium applying in a period and being somewhat dependent on previous equilibria, as well as on anticipations about future equilibria. This vision inspired the teaching of A. Marshall and the reflections of the Swedish school. It has been formalized since then, particularly by Hicks in *Value and Capital* (1939) and subsequent writings.

The crux of this vision lies in the general features of what is called 'the temporary equilibrium'. Within a period agents are engaged in economic activities and in particular trade with each other. Each agent is in a situation that results from the past; he or she forms anticipations about the future of the economy, chooses or at least reconsiders his or her plans on the basis of observed present opportunities; he or she acts in conformity with these plans. Moreover the actions of the various agents are made mutually consistent; at the very least new contracts involving two parties must be accepted by both and agree with their respective plans.

Within this framework many possibilities exist for more specific theories, depending on what is assumed about economic structures, the activities of agents, the way in which they form their anticipations and their behaviour, the trading opportunities and the consistency that is realized in each period. But this framework serves to organize observation and reflection, as well as to draw first conclusions. I shall not insist on the fact that the national accounts in particular are set up exactly in conformity with the framework. I must rather consider the fact that within this framework no single theory exists, which would simultaneously deal with all aspects of macroeconomic phenomena.

(ii) The project to build such a unified theory inspired many people who dreamed about the ideal. It is still present today, even though theoreticians may be reluctant to exhibit ambitions that might look too immodest. It appears in particular in one conception of what the microeconomic foundations of macroeconomics ought to be: not, as I think they are, separate justifications given to different macroeconomic hypotheses, but a grand microeconomic theory from which all macroeconomic theories would be derived by different processes of aggregation and simplification (see for instance Weintraub, 1985).

Clearly this all-purpose theory is not available today. We have one well-developed neoclassical theory of growth, which is appropriate to deal with many aspects of economic growth, but not with all of them. We have a theory of short-term employment equilibrium, which today encompasses more than when Keynes introduced it but which nevertheless deals only with the short term. We have a few theories of inflation, which one might hope to unify, and so on. Experts in charge of diagnosis then have to use partial theoretical and empirical models, which experience has shown to be appropriate for the study of various aspects of phenomena.

Before we look more precisely into some of the main theoretical systems now used and into some improvements that might hopefully be brought to them, let me say again that the lack of unity of the available theory is neither likely to be soon removed nor specific to economics. It will not be removed quickly because, as soon as one wants to extend the range of phenomena to which a theory applies, one discovers that this theory has not been fully worked out even for those phenomena it was supposed to cover; one then has to work more deeply into the old confines; this work raises new problems not considered so far, and so on. Often even the intention to extend the range of application of the theory disappears in the process.

Moreover, a similar lack of unity characterizes all disciplines that now have to deal with complex systems or complex organisms, and the economic system is certainly complex. In biology also each aspect of the phenomena, being mainly determined by particular structures or functions, is approached by a particular branch using specific simplified models and specific experimental tools with little integration between branches (metabolic biochemistry, molecular biology, cellular physiology, general physiology etc.). Hence, economists should not be afraid of being found eclectic. Rather be eclectic and approximately right in various applications, than dogmatic and often wrong. This was well expressed by Professor Caffé who, quoting Samuelson, stated that in economics, eclecticism was a necessity (Caffé, 1986, p. 9).

(iii) The major paradigm used in macroeconomic diagnosis is undoubtedly the Keynesian one, as it was developed during several decades, in particular for and by the construction of national and international macroeconometric models. The core remains a theory of short-term employment in which market disequilibria play an important role. Diagnosis concerning the short-term evolution of output and employment has to identify and measure the disequilibria, as well as their trends; in order to provide better forecasts than pure extrapolations, it has to explain these disequilibria.

Over the past fifteen years it has become fashionable to express doubts about Keynesian theory and its developments. The truth is, however, that it continues to be the main reference used in applications, even sometimes by people who were among the most vocal critics when in academic circles but who later became government experts. For those theoreticians who recognize the usefulness and appropriateness of this theory when dealing with macroeconomic diagnosis at the horizon of one to a few years, the main task should be to make it more robust and still more appropriate. This purpose has led and may still lead to many research projects, about which lack of space prevents me from commenting. I just want to stress here the two research objectives to which I should like to give priority.

First one should examine how direct observation on disequilibria ought best to be made part of the models used in practice. This observation always played an important role in diagnosis but was somewhat neglected in the macroeconometric models built in the 1960s and 1970s, except for the presence of the unemloyment rate. Attempts to fully integrate direct observation of disequilibria now exist (see in particular Lambert, 1988), but still remain at an experimental stage.

Second the representation of the supply of goods and services ought to be reconsidered, so as to make the models more suitable for the study of the medium run. Such important aspects of medium-term evolution as non-price competitiveness or the building of productive capacity, to be distinguished from productive investment, play too small a role in our current models. These aspects may be difficult to analyse and even to characterize properly; but they are valuable challenges for research.

(iv) A good deal of the time devoted to diagnosis by experts concerns inflation. It seems to me that the main teaching of macroeconomics gives an inaccurate view of this work because it conveys the idea of a fully unified theory, dealing at the same time with inflation and output or employment. I certainly do not want to argue that prices and production obey two different systems that are independent from one another. But the process of evolution of the general price level and the growth process each have enough specific aspects for a deep study of one to be often made with reference to only some general features of the other. This is why I believe it would in many cases be more correct to consider that we work with two theories, one dealing with inflation, the other with employment – two theories with some overlap but not fully integrated with one another.

A few facts about inflation have been well identified: the role of expectations, their dependence with respect to past evolution, hence the inertia of the process; the role of demand pressure, both on the market for labour and on the market for goods; the role of wage bargaining, which sometimes involves government; the role of the prices of basic imported energy and materials, even that of domestic agricultural prices. The problem in applications comes from the lack of accuracy with which these various elements and their interplay are known. As for me I see no other way of making progress than by repeated econometric studies of the many cases that experience in various countries provides us with. This is bound to be laborious, but will give better results than the alternative of accepting for inflation diagnosis a simple hypothesis, such as the quantity theory of money.

(v) I must refer here to yet a third kind of macroeconomic theory, the one dealing with medium to long-run growth. The problem in this respect is different. We have a well formalized theory of economic growth, a theory that has many versions from the ones given by Solow and neoclassical mathematical economists having worked at a lower level of aggregation, to the ones due to von Neumann and to followers of Sraffa. Except for distinctions interesting only specialists, these various versions provide about the same service, namely to help in tracing the interdependence between the evolutions of major aggregates concerning quantities, relative prices and real remuneration rates. The problem is that this theory says very little about the forces that drive economic growth.

This theory is now the subject of a new interest motivated precisely by the wish to extend its relevance for macroeconomics (see Romer, 1986). By modelling increasing returns to scale in research and innovative activities, one hopes to understand better how saving can contribute to growth. This new development is most welcome and will certainly bear fruit, although, I am afraid, fruit that will be less important than some of its proponents claim.

But the main problem will remain, namely for us to achieve a better grasp of what Schumpeter stressed: the role of the entre-preneur and the conditions under which this role expands. Intuition tells us that flexibility in economic organization is one condition for it; but what is then meant precisely by flexibility? Intuition also tells us that there are virtuous circles in which an initial profitability advantage has contributed to generate competitiveness, hence high profitability. But such favourable disequilibrium processes have not been well formalized so far, and while it may be easy to speak of them ex post, we do not yet really know how to assess their future in practice. This is a real challenge and I should like to see some younger economists trying to face it.

References

B. Balassa et al. (1971), *The Structure of Protection in Developing Countries*, Johns Hopkins University Press, Baltimore.

B. Balassa et al. (1982), *Development Strategies in Semi-Industrial Countries*, Johns Hopkins University Press, Baltimore.

F. Caffé (1986), *In difesa del 'Welfare state': soggi di politica economica*, Rosenberge Sellier, Turin.

S. Grossman and J. Stiglitz (1980), 'On the impossibility of informationally efficient markets', *American Economic Review*, 70, pp. 393–408.

J. Hicks (1939), *Value and Capital*, Clarendon Press, Oxford.

J. Jordan and R. Radner (1982), 'Rational expectations in microeconomic models: an overview', *Journal of Economic Theory*, 26, pp. 201–23.

J.-P. Lambert (1988), *Disequilibrium Macroeconomic Models*, Cambridge University Press, Cambridge.

J.B. Nelson and C.I. Plosser (1982), 'Trends and random walks in macroeconomic time series: some evidence and implications', *Journal of Monetary Economics*, 10, pp. 139–69.

P. Romer (1986), 'Increasing returns and long-run growth', *Journal of Political Economy*, 94, pp. 1002–37.

E.R. Weintraub (1985), *General Equilibrium Analysis: Studies in Appraisal*, Cambridge University Press, Cambridge.

2

Analysis and forecasting: their respective roles in mastering our destinies

1. Introduction

Man is concerned about the future and hence ready to listen to anyone claiming to forecast. Foretellers have always had a credulous audience. The rapid development of science and the esteem with which it is regarded have not been enough to make this divinatory activity disappear.

This is because man is in a hurry; he feels a strong urge to know what tomorrow will be like: to understand before forecasting would take much too long. In fact, many believe in forecasts which are not really based on a true understanding of the phenomena in question.

Today, I would like to urge the participants of this symposium to beware of the attitude that treats forecasting as an autonomous discipline. Forecasting would only be truly autonomous if it could be separated from understanding phenomena. Conscious of being provocative, I may say that the main *raison d'être* of an autonomous science of forecasting, if it was built, could well be to justify resorting to foretellers.

I will on the contrary defend the thesis that a thorough analysis of phenomena is the true source of progress in the art of forecasting. My talk will contain three parts. In the first part I shall claim that forecasting without theory is rarely efficient and therefore studying forecasting methodology as such can only play a rather limited role in improving forecasts. In the second part I shall consider modelling, which formalizes our theories about the phenomenon under study, and which lends support to forecasting; I shall then indicate how the reliability of modelling depends mostly on the effort

Translated by Fatemeh Shadman-Mehta. Keynote speech at the Sixth International Symposium of Forecasting, Paris, June 1986; published in French in *International Journal of Forecasting*, 3 (1987), pp. 187–94.

originally spent on analytically acquiring knowledge. In the third part, I shall start from the fact that forecasts exist, sometimes even beyond justification; I will then ask which common principles, applicable to all scientific disciplines, ought to be observed in order to ensure that forecasting activity is carried out correctly and usefully. In sum, the question raised will be that of the ethics of forecasting.

2. Forecasting is rarely possible without theory

The observation of past regularities is certainly sufficient at times to make reliable extrapolations of the future. The succession of days and seasons was very well forecast, long before the Earth's movement was understood.

As you all know, one can make a rigorous analysis of how to go from observation to forecasting within the framework of the theory of stochastic processes. By observing a process over a long period, we can 'know' it, that is we can estimate its properties. Good forecasts are possible if the estimation is precise. Even if estimation is precise, the forecast itself is not necessarily precise because the innovation component of the process may be substantial. But an 'optimal forecast' can be obtained by taking due account of the costs implied by forecast errors. Appropriate formulae have already been developed for many types of stochastic processes using a methodology which is now quite old (Wiener, 1949; Kalman, 1960; Box and Jenkins, 1970).

Unfortunately, the cases where this methodology is sufficient are rare. Yet again, the difficulty of the problem often does not lie in the forecasting phase to which routine procedures are now applicable. The difficulty lies in the estimation phase, or rather in the phase of elucidating what structure a given process could possibly have. The case recurring most frequently is the one where direct and clear observation only reveals chaotic movement to begin with.

I have neither the competence nor the time necessary to describe here the most frequent situations in different scientific domains, or the way specialists in each domain choose to work in order to achieve a better forecasting acuteness. But I can briefly recount the development of ideas in economics, which is certainly not an abnormal case and presents an interest of its own.

During the years between the two world wars, and we won't go any further into the past, a lot of effort was devoted, especially in the United States, to promoting the observation of economic regularities and this in particular with forecasting purposes in mind. The 'Harvard barometer' was destined to announce in advance major economic changes. An ambitious research programme had begun at the National Bureau of Economic Research (NBER), under the impetus of Professor W. Mitchell, with the aim of empirically identifying economic cycles so as to be able to forecast them (the best account of this research is in the large book by Burns and Mitchell, 1946). Those economists most interested in methodology were beginning to concentrate their attention on the statistical analysis of time series (Tintner, 1940; Davis, 1941).

All this activity gave place to an intense effort of reflection during the Second World War and the years immediately after the war, which led to the rejection of NBER methodology and the emergence of a new methodology defined by the Cowles Commission, a research group based at the University of Chicago (the best summary of these debates is undoubtedly found in the exchange between Koopmans and Vining published in the *Review of Economics and Statistics* in 1947 and 1949 and reproduced in Gordon and Klein, 1966). According to this new methodology, in order to understand and be able to forecast the simultaneous changes in the various magnitudes, it was advisable to study them within a system of structural equations. Each equation was to represent either one of the various types of behaviour or one of the many market adjustments which together constitute the economic system. For instance, one equation would express the way firms' investments are determined, while another would explain how average wage rates vary. The statistical estimation was not to be aimed immediately at studying the properties of the values taken by each of the more interesting magnitudes taken on their own. It had to look at the complete structural system, which would be made up of relationships with their own particular form, and containing enough exogenous variables acting upon one or the other section of the economic system (see for example Hood and Koopmans, 1953).

The impulse thus given to econometric research forty years ago, has since been pursued in more or less the way it was laid out. We recognize its most visible manifestation: various teams all over the world, in administrations, central banks, universities or independent organizations, have developed macroeconometric models of their countries, faithfully applying the methodology conceived at the Cowles Commission. These models, which are at times applied to annual series and at times to quarterly series, are often large models of up to thousands of equations. They provide macro-economic forecasts which are studied and closely analysed by the most diverse authorities.

Being aware of the fact that on the one hand economic science is not very advanced, and that on the other it is the subject of important debates between opposing schools of thought, one cannot help but be overwhelmed at this prolonged quasi-unanimity. Three remarks are called for in the context of this symposium.

First, we must recognize that each macroeconomic model reflects a theory about how an economic system functions. Judging a model is not simply a matter of examining whether it is correctly specified from a statistical point of view, that is whether the estimation of its many parameters is properly based on all the series describing the past development of the magnitudes under study. One must also question the theoretical validity of the specification. Such an examination might not appear as very crucial, given that most models belong to the same theoretical family. Their core represents various components of demand for goods as well as rather traditional laws regarding the determination of income. Nevertheless, economic theory is always present; we are still far removed from the purely empirical option of stochastic processes and their forecasts.

Second, the forecasting accuracy of the methodology is not as good as one would have hoped. It is unnecessary to comment at great length on this remark, although the point has to be made. It undoubtedly reveals the somewhat erratic nature of economic phenomena even more than the ambiguities in our economic theories. Nevertheless, these mediocre forecasts are still clearly superior to those obtained from pure extrapolation (Zarnowitz, 1978; Fonteneau, 1982).

Third, although the methodology of the Cowles Commission is widely followed, economists themselves are nowadays questioning this methodology to some extent. This doubt, which was always latently present, found a new life with the article by Sims (1980) entitled 'Macroeconomics and reality' in which he also calls for a much more empirical alternative methodology.

Sims' critique addresses the arbitrariness of many of the hypotheses maintained by econometricians when specifying models by which they claim to put forward their theories. His recommendation is essentially to go back to time-series techniques of analysis and forecasting, but applying them to a few series simultaneously, that is by considering the multidimensional stochastic processes generating them. In short, the only contribution of economic theory would be to guide the choice of the main series to consider simultaneously (this choice is obviously of crucial importance).

The critique is certainly sound and the recommendation leads to interesting applications. For a long time economists have neglected data analysis which would help familiarization with available observations. They have too often neglected comparing the results of their sophisticated models with those obtained from a much more empirical approach such as advocated by Sims and others like him. Personally speaking, I study results obtained with this alternative methodology with great care.

In the final analysis, however, I believe that the usual methodology comes out of such comparisons the strongest. Accuracy achieved by Sims and his school remains very poor, almost as poor as what researchers at the NBER used to achieve. Given that their method directly allows for simultaneous consideration of only up to six series, one is forced either to make highly dubious assumptions about the independence of these particular series from the rest of the economic system, or to introduce highly arbitrary ad hoc assumptions in order to reduce the dimension of the stochastic process covering a larger number of series. In the latter case, the difference with the usual methodology is that existing economic theory plays no part in the choice of the additional assumptions. In other words, one ignores the stock of thought and confrontation with facts which has been gradually built up by economic theory.

3. Methodical detailed analysis matters

In short, to ensure the quality of economic forecasts, the most important thing is to have a good model representation of economic phenomena. I have just stated that such modelling can only be the outcome of a slow scientific accumulation, involving many detailed studies. Economics is not unique in this respect either. This brings me to the second part of my overview. At this stage I would like to convince you that modelling requires analysis; it often even requires a whole range of preliminary works of different nature, some based on abstract reflection, some seeking factual observations, some combining both.

The forecaster may sometimes encounter the favourable circumstances of being expected to outline the results of the functioning of a system that can be directly modelled. This would be the case, for example, for a mechanical system designed by engineers. It is also the case of a functional organization which stipulates precisely the allocation of roles in a collective activity. In such situations, the direct application of system analysis is appropriate. Simplifications will certainly be necessary to arrive at a practical model; even so, one will need to use simulations or approximations to arrive at a solution. But all this is feasible thanks to the usual techniques of system analysis.

Most of the time, however, the situation is much less favourable. The system is imperfectly known and imperfectly mastered. In general, the theory about the phenomenon under study only indicates the broad structure of the system governing it without clarifying the details. Even if one assumed that this theory was well established and little contested, which is clearly not always the case, there is still a long way to go before a model is built which can be used for forecasting.

In other words, the common situation is one where we know the nature of the main blocks of the model as well as the nature of their mutual relationships. But many questions remain open as regards their detailed specification. At a certain moment, the forecaster who cannot wait will fix his or her model as well as possible, by choosing options more or less arbitrarily, more or less skilfully.

Hence, it is clear that improvement of forecasting accuracy requires better knowledge of the most uncertain blocks and the least well-defined relations, at least those that have a greater influence on forecasts.

Let us once again consider an example. Suppose we want to forecast French unemployment. Given that unemployment at its present level reflects global disequilibrium between labour supply and demand, the structure of the model must include two large blocks, one of which determines labour supply and the other labour demand. The change in unemployment is obtained from the difference between the increase in supply and the increase in demand. A serious consideration of each block's specification reveals many questions. To answer those questions one must refer to various theoretical studies, which are either completed or are to be undertaken. Let us limit ourselves to labour demand.

Firms' demand for labour depends on output growth and changes in methods of production. A good model for forecasting labour demand must therefore explain properly the level of output on the one hand, and changes in production techniques on the other. Many factors need to be taken into account for both aspects. But our present theory only provides incomplete information on how to do it. In other words, the two sub-blocks that determine output and the quantity of labour per unit of output will have specific structures resulting from what we already know. But to choose the specification more precisely involves choices for which we feel the need to be better informed. I will not evoke all these choices. But to demonstrate their crucial role, I will limit myself to one particular question.

One of the clearest changes in the economic environment of French enterprises is that the real cost of labour has ceased to grow rapidly. This cost, which had increased much more than productivity ever since the first oil shock, has now been practically constant for the last three years. It is widely believed that in the present French situation and over the medium term, this change is favourable to employment despite the fact that it has also slowed down the growth of households' purchasing power. A good forecasting model of labour demand in France must properly reflect the role played by the real cost of labour. Economists and econometricians have views on this subject which cannot be ignored. But these views are also highly imprecise; only specific and painstaking studies can help to clarify them.

The observed change in the cost of labour signals on the one hand that firms' profitability is being restored, and on the other hand that there is a clear break in the growth of cost of labour relative to capital. As profitability is restored, firms' hesitancy to start new projects, that is to invest, should disappear. And as these projects reach completion, our firms will be in a position to increase their presence in markets, gradually regain competitiveness, and hence produce more and employ at a faster rate.

The break in the growth of the relative cost of labour also means that while getting the most out of technological progress, when reviewing their production techniques and choosing their investment firms will less systematically attempt to reduce the use of labour. This should also lead to a gradual reversal of current trends.

The proper measurement of all the phenomena I have just mentioned, whose effects as you have gathered are spread over many years, is crucial for forecasting employment, and hence unemployment, accurately. Unfortunately, the relationships representing these phenomena involve a number of coefficients about which we know little (I discussed this question recently in an explanatory rather than a forecasting context; see Malinvaud, 1986). Therefore, what is required is an arduous programme of econometric studies without any certainty that such a programme will be successful.

If I could have devoted more time to this example, I would have shown how it reveals not only the fact that preliminary studies are of the utmost importance for elaborating forecasting models, but also the nature of the process they must follow. It is not original to note that the process involves to-ings and fro-ings between theoretical reflection and experimentation, or seeking lessons from observations. In fields such as economics, theoretical reflection must clarify among other things how to aggregate, that is how to move from microeconomics to macroeconomics.

In sum, anyone working in a particular scientific domain has the feeling that forecasting is an end product. It is even an easy end product compared to the long and hard, often even disappointing work which is necessary for the gradual improvement of knowledge.

4. Forecasting must be a disciplined activity

I have just examined the broad outlines of the necessary conditions for producing the best possible forecasts in a given state of knowledge. I still need to bring to your attention how the exercise of forecasting is integrated in our society. All is not well in this respect. My message is simple: in every discipline, forecasting must be a disciplined activity; it must be subject to the norms of scientific work; it must even be integrated into the scientific work programmes of which it is an element.

Let us begin by noting that basic scientific research, which plays the most important part in improving our forecasting abilities, often suffers because demand for forecasts is too pressing. In our modern media societies, we are all asked to formulate forecasts and some of us are even harassed. An occasional demand can sometimes prompt useful stimulation. What happens more frequently, however, is that demand is so pressing that it plays a detrimental role.

Indeed, the temptation to respond is there, even if the reply cannot be as reliable as it is more or less implicitly assumed to be. There is then a real risk that the scientist may deviate from the scientific norms that ought to be respected. There is also a real risk that this may bring fame which would not have been had otherwise. And finally there is a real risk that the scientist might thus benefit in the allocation of resources for scientific research. One can easily imagine the kind of aberrations that may result. Hence, over-insistent demands for forecasts can be detrimental to scientific progress and ultimately to the control of our destinies.

To protect against the risk of such deviations, scientists in each discipline must promote in their own ranks professional ethics of forecasting, and ensure that such ethics are respected. It is not difficult to define their main principles: forecasts should not be intentionally misleading, forecasts should be competently produced, using the appropriate stock of knowledge and the best available techniques. (They could be misleading either by being intentionally biased or by hiding their degree of uncertainty and they could be incompetently produced either if they result from a crude procedure, or if they ignore scientific results which are likely to affect them.)

The development of professional ethics of forecasting in each discipline helps that particular scientific community in better achieving its mission and improving its knowledge. It can also directly serve the whole society, which can better recognize and distinguish serious forecasts made by specialists from those made by unqualified persons, firms or organizations. If they do their work properly, journalists will easily distinguish and abstain from publicizing poor-quality forecasts.

It is clearly not for me to indicate how ethics of forecasting are to be established in each discipline. In French economic administrations it has emerged and taken shape out of a collective awakening. This awakening has benefited from lessons drawn from incidents or difficulties with public authorities, or from public presentations. The professional code addresses more generally the projections which serve not only in making forecasts, but also in determining the expected effects of different variants of economic policy. It means the obligation to clarify publicly the method used in making the projections and its limits, as well as the inherent assumptions. (Although such a code of ethics has not been completely explained in print, it shows through in Dubois, 1981 in particular.)

However, I can say that generally speaking, one element of the professional ethics of forecasting must be ex-post comparisons of past forecasts with what has happened in reality. A forecasting error is not proof in itself that the forecast was badly made, or even that it played no useful role. But past errors, and possibly some reasons explaining them, ought to be recognized.

The usefulness of an ex-post study of forecasts goes well beyond the development of professional ethics. Such a study is an integral part of a scientific approach. There is no doubt that a comparison of forecasts versus realizations never has the same convincing value as a controlled experiment; the assumptions made about some exogenous factors can never be verified exactly, thus greatly complicating the lessons to be drawn from the comparison. Nevertheless, when experimentation is impossible – in other words in areas where factual observations on phenomena are only obtained from the observation of events or developments which are not constructed by researchers – comparison of forecasts with realizations does not intrinsically have less potential than estimations, tests or other operations which are carried out most frequently.

It is, however, unusual to see forecasts made solely for the purpose of comparing with results. The main purpose of forecasts is rather to lead to more lucid action, whenever the results will be affected by events or developments to be forecast. There are many examples of cases where easily predictable events or developments have been ignored in decision-making, and then some aspects of those decisions, or even the decisions *in toto*, have later been regretted. To make more rational choices, it is essential to develop the habit of making forecasts as rigorous as possible and in good time. (In my particular field, I have had occasion to examine the usefulness of forecasts made by macroeconomists; see Malinvaud, 1981.)

All in all, forecasting must be distinguished from science. Only science can achieve progress in knowledge, a progress which is crucial to the control of our destinies. But forecasting is one of the exercises, one of the arts by which we must put our knowledge into practice for a better mastery of our destinies.

References

G.E.P. Box and G.M. Jenkins (1970), *Time Series Analysis, Forecasting and Control*, Holden Day, San Francisco.

A.F. Burns and W.C. Mitchell (1946), *Measuring Business Cycles*, National Bureau of Economic Research, New York.

H. Davis (1941), *The Analysis of Economic Time Series*, Principia Press, Bloomington, IN.

P. Dubois (1981), 'L'INSEE met ses modèles à la disposition des utilisateurs non administratifs', *Courrier des Statistiques*, 17.

A. Fonteneau (1982), 'La fiabilité des prévisions macroéconomiques à court terme: 12 ans d'expériences françaises (1970–1981)', *Observations et diagnostics économiques*, 2.

R.A. Gordon and L.R. Klein (1966) (eds.), *Readings in Business Cycles*, Allen & Unwin, London.

W.C. Hood and T.C. Koopmans (1953) (eds.), *Studies in Econometric Methods*, Wiley, New York.

R.E. Kalman (1960), 'A new approach to linear filtering and prediction problems', *Journal of Basic Engineering*, D82.

E. Malinvaud (1981), 'Econometrics faced with the needs of macroeconomic policy', *Econometrica*, 49, pp. 1363–75.

(1986), 'Les causes de la montée du chômage en France', *Revue française d'économie* 1, pp. 50–83 ('The rise of unemployment in France', *Economica*, 53, Supplement, pp. 198–217).

C. Sims (1980), 'Macroeconomics and reality', *Econometrica*, 48, pp. 1–48.

G. Tintner (1940), *The Variate Difference Method*, Bloomington Press, Bloomington, IN.

N. Wiener (1949), *Extrapolation, Interpolation and Smoothing of Stationary Time Series*, Wiley, New York.

V. Zarnowitz (1978), 'On the accuracy and properties of recent macroeconomic forecasts', *American Economic Review*, 68(2), pp. 313, 319.

3

From statistics to projections

Quantitative projections are based on statistics, their sophistication being often constrained by unavailability of data. They rely on a representation of the structure of the phenomenon and in particular of its dynamics. In many applications the model may appear rather simplistic, the main difficulty being the appropriate choice of variables. When modelization requires statistical inference, structural and dynamic aspects are often both relevant, their proper interplay raising delicate issues.

Surveying the use of statistics for projections in the socio-economic field, this lecture will aim at stimulating reflection on present practices, so as eventually to contribute to their improvement. Some of the most important projections will be first reviewed; the need for better statistical data will then be considered before the role of analytical statistical inference. Section 4 will be devoted to a discussion about the important issue of choosing where to put the main emphasis: on the structural or the dynamic aspects of the phenomenon. This survey moreover raises questions of a fundamental nature about scientific methodology on social and economic matters, questions that will be approached in the concluding section.

1. Projection practices

A full survey of present projection practices would exhibit their great diversity, even when attention is limited to the socio-economic field. In order to focus the discussion here, only some of them, dealing with population and the economy, will be briefly reviewed.

Delatour Lecture, International Statistical Institute, Tokyo, September 1987; published in French in *Bulletin de l'Institut International de Statistique* (46th session), Tokyo, 1987.

Demographic projections have for many years been on the agenda of the United Nations Secretariat that has issued many of them,[1] and a series of manuals as well.[2] The methodology was widely discussed by experts both before and after the elaboration of the main manuals.[3] Considering two important applications of this methodology is safely looking at some of the best present practices. I shall add a third example of population projection drawn from French works.

The basis for the demographic prospects issued by UN is the projection by sex/age groups, this resulting from the so called 'component method': trends of mortality, fertility and migration are independently forecast after an analysis of past levels and trends, supplemented by explicit assumptions. The work is being consistently done with a decomposition by age and sex; several sets of assumptions are applied, leading to as many projections.

For instance in the last set of projections, it is assumed that, during each five-year period, there is a gain in life expectancy at birth of 2.5 years up to an expectancy of 62.5 years, the gain progressively slowing down beyond this point; this general assumption about mortality trends is, however, revised for countries in which recent evidence indicates a retardation or an acceleration by comparision with the main pattern. Three alternative variants of fertility assumptions are being made; anticipated changes in the socio-economic structure and cultural values of the society, as well as policies and programmes directed towards family planning, are considered vis-à-vis expected trends in fertility. As for international migrations, it is assumed that their net flow for each country will progressively move to zero as time passes, except for those countries for which the evidence strongly suggests a continuation of current migration levels for a considerable time into the future.

The UN projections of the largest cities of the world were widely publicized and commented (United Nations, 1980). They are built in two steps. First, the evolution of the urban population of the country is forecast on the basis of the global projections just discussed and of an extrapolation of the urban/rural growth

---

[1] See for instance United Nations (1985).

[2] See in particular: Manual III: *Methods for Population Projections by Sex and Age*; Manual V: *Methods of Projecting the Economically Active Population*; Manual VII: *Methods of Projecting Households and Families*, Manual VIII: *Methods for Projections of Urban and Rural Population*.

[3] See for instance United Nations (1979).

difference (the excess of the urban over the rural growth rate is assumed to be in the future a weighted mean of the difference most recently observed in the country and of the difference that would be implied by a pattern fitted on 110 countries, according to which this difference is a declining linear function of the urban proportion already reached; the weights more and more favour the general pattern as one moves into a more distant future). The second step proceeds to an extrapolation of the difference between the growth rates of the particular city considered and of the urban population of the country (exactly the same kind of extrapolation is assumed as for the urban/rural growth difference; a correction is, however, made in countries in which the growth rate of all cities aggregated is found to exceed the growth rate of the urban population, the correction then has the effect of dampening the phenomenon).

The future growth of the foreign population expected to live in France was recently the subject of hot debate; INSEE then thought it had to provide objective demographic projections in this respect (Labat and Dekneudt, 1986). (To be frank, one must recognize that the real concern was often more on ethnicity than on nationality; but this was hardly ever made explicit, since ethnic differences were traditionally asserted not to matter in France and are not recorded in French statistics.) Starting from the foreign population living in France at the time of the 1982 census, broken down by nationality, sex, age and place of birth (France or abroad), the 'survival rates' observed between the 1975 and 1982 censuses are applied for estimates of those parts of these foreign populations that will remain in France in 1989 (the decrease covers deaths, emigrations and nationality changes, three components that cannot be separately estimated by lack of appropriate data). Entry of foreign workers is assumed (two hypotheses are made, one assuming the same numbers as observed between 1975 and 1982, the other assuming a decrease). Observed patterns are used for projecting entry of relatives (depending on the disequilibrium between the male and female populations living in France) and foreign births in France (depending on fertility rates estimated separately for three categories of women: born in France, born abroad but living in France in 1982, to enter France between 1982 and 1989). The same kind of projections are repeated for 1996, 2003 and 2010.

In the economic field, macroeconomic projections are the most widely known. No other kind will be discussed here, although it is also in business practice to forecast the trend of sales for major products. Methods commonly used for macroeconomic projections are by now fairly standard. Roughly described, they belong to three main categories, which I may call 'informed assessment of likely trends', 'projection based on a macroeconometric model' and 'vector autoregressive extrapolation'.

As a good representative of the first method, OECD's semi-annual economic outlook may be considered.[4] It aims at producing countries' forecasts that are consistent externally as well as internally. To ensure international consistency, the OECD's INTER-LINK system is used at all stages; this system draws the quantitative material prepared by the country and general specialists into an integrated simulation system. Country specialists try to best take into account available specific information but also all rely on the same well-recognized economic relations, such as the dependence of private consumption on real personal disposable income, or of price changes on cost changes and on demand conditions. Particular attention is given to the forecasts concerning international trade, as well as import and export prices, great use being then made of the structural equations embodied in the INTERLINK system. The forecasts are conditional upon a set of technical assumptions, such as exchange rates remaining constant and stated national policies being applied.

The use of macroeconometrics is more systematic in the second method in which projections are directly computed by an integrated model, whose equations have all been fitted on the same base of macroeconomic time series. The nature of these models is so well known that it need not be described again here;[5] but a few comments about their use for projections may be in order. As an example, I may refer to the medium-term projections made in France on the basis of the DMS model operating at INSEE (Fouquet et al., 1978; Guillaume and Muet, 1979; Bianchi et al., 1984). The method is, indeed, more strictly applied for projections to, say, five years than for short-term projections, which always incorporate in practice outside information even when they are model based (some equation is considered as not applying during

---

[4] The forecasting techniques used are described in the 'Sources and Methods' chapter that is annexed to the presentation of economic projections. See for instance OECD (1986).

[5] See for instance Intriligator (1978), Fair (1984), Artus et al. (1986).

the coming year, or an exceptional shock is taken for granted, and so on); because of such a practice the difference from the first method is then small. But of course medium-term projections are more demanding and cannot be expected to be very accurate (French projections made from DMS, however, turned out to be much better than the informal forecasts usually heard when they were issued). By comparison with the first method, use of macro-econometric models is more transparent, less discretionary, more appropriate for the learning process involving ex-post assessment of the value of past projections; this feature is reinforced if, as is done in France, two functions are explicitly separated and performed by different teams: the choice of future values to be given to the main exogenous variables, the building, upkeep and operation of the macroeconometric model.

Such models, however, are considered as too specific by the few advocates of a third method amounting to extrapolation of a multidimensional stochastic process fitted on a few important macroeconomic time series (Sims, 1980; Doan et al., 1984). This method has few adepts in applied macroeconomics, because it is believed to assume too much autonomy for the evolution of the few variables of interest and it neglects what is known about the impact coming from other variables. It is, however, worth mentioning here, since it belongs to the family of widely promoted methods of time-series extrapolation that are also found useful in other cases of socio-economic projections (Box and Jenkins, 1970).

When reflecting on the present projection practices, which the cases presented above probably portray accurately, statisticians are led to raise at least four questions. Is the data base good enough for projections and how could it be improved? What should be the role of statistical inference in the preliminary stages leading to the choice of a model? In formalized projections, how best to combine considerations of the dynamic and structural aspects of the phenomenon? What are more generally the philosophical requirements for an objective assessment of future trends in the socio-economic field? These four questions will be considered in turn in the four following sections.

2. Relevant data

Clearly, many cases can be found in which the accuracy of the data base used in projections leaves much to be desired. For instance, the group of experts that met at UN in 1977 on demographic projections stated that 'the majority of developing countries lack adequate current data on which to base population projections'. In developed countries also some population projections may significantly suffer from the inaccuracy of the data. For instance, French censuses probably miss some part of the foreign population living in the country, notwithstanding the special efforts made for achieving a good coverage in this respect; this part may not have been the same in the two censuses taken in 1975 and 1982; so, for the foreign population projections reported above, both the picture of the initial situation and the estimate of the survival rates may be the sources of significant bias. Similarly, in the economic field, projections mainly rely on the series of national accounts; but most developing countries have no proper accounts, or have them on a consistent base for only a few years; experts know also that in developed countries parts of existing national accounts are weak. All this means that all countries still have to invest in their official statistics if they want to improve the quality of their socio-economic projections.

One ought to go beyond this rather trivial observation and be more specific. Here I shall only consider one problem, maybe the major one: in many cases the most relevant variables are simply not observed, which results in reliance on a very crude model or on quite imperfect proxies. For instance for the French projection of foreign populations, mortality rates and emigration rates by nationality were not available, neither did one know all acquisitions of French nationality; this is why one had to rely on survival rates covering the combined result of these three quite distinct phenomena; improvement of the projections would then require a serious extension and refinement of existing statistics.

For economic projections the major lacuna lies in the common unavailability of national wealth accounts that would complement the familiar national accounts dealing with current operations and be articulated with them. This creates a serious difficulty for the assessment of the impact and evolution of such loosely recognized factors of future growth as indebtedness of firms, governments or nations. Similarly the role to be given to the profitability of various types of operation tends to be neglected, because good measures of profit rates are not commonly available and would require appropriate wealth accounts.

It is worth noting that, since working on projections reveals significant gaps in existing statistics, close connection with statistical offices may assist in the proper orientation of investments in official statistics. Indeed, examples are easily found where the stimulus coming from this origin can be identified. For instance the input–output methodology, used for tracing future industrial trends, required a higher degree of consistency between classifications by types of commodity and types of industry; this gave its rationale to the work done on these classifications both at the national and international levels. Similarly, early involvement of French statisticians in the projections of employment broken down by professional groups, of requirements addressed to the education system and of social mobility explains very well why so much attention was given in France to the emergence and systematic use of a classification by professions and socio-professional categories that is recognized as a kind of model. Work on national wealth accounts is also particularly promoted in the countries where close collaboration exists between statisticians and economists concerned with analysis and projections.

3. Learning from statistical inference

To the extent that they reveal something about real phenomena, all kinds of statistical inference are of course valuable for projections. It might not be necessary to say more here if the consequences of this obvious remark were always seriously taken into account. But they are often neglected by promoters of mechanical methods of forecasting. One must on the contrary strongly stress that the quality of most projections mainly depends not only on the accuracy of the data base but also on the advancement of the scientific analysis of the phenomena involved. In order to be a little more specific while insisting on this truth, I will briefly consider three important research aims: detection of relevant categories, detection of main factors of a phenomenon, detection of trend changes.

It is clear from the examples reported above that many projections rely on typologies defining the elementary categories to be used in the computations. In some cases the criteria defining the categories are obvious, such as sex and age in the main demographic projections. In other cases the best criteria may have to be found. Indeed, both the general work on classifications mentioned in the previous section and the choice of the categories to be used in a particular projection can benefit from statistical inference on the groupings that best discriminate with respect to the relevant aspects of the phenomenon.

Already with the projections of population of large cities, an intermediate breakdown of the country population into the urban and rural was used. What should have been the best dividing line between the two? Was this kind of breakdown the best one to be used for an intermediate stage? These questions are not easily answered, but thinking over them suggests that a simple urban–rural dichotomy provides only a very rough distinction. A data analysis of the socio-professional composition of the 36,000 French communes distinguishes thirty-five types, which for a first approximation may be aggregated into four broad groups (Tabard, 1985). It is moreover found that these thirty-five types are quite discriminating with respect to population trends, with annual growth rates in the last period of observation varying from −2 to +9 per cent.

Detection of the main factors of a phenomenon and quanitification of their effects is of course essential for a good assessment of the future evolution of the phenomenon. Consider for instance an attempt at forecasting unemployment trends in the various Western European countries. This may be viewed as an output of macro-economic projections and therefore as depending on a good understanding of all aspects of economic growth. But many of these aspects are still poorly understood. For instance the potential role of a European 'wage gap' has been scrutinized for some years but no general agreement has yet been reached about it. Roughly speaking (although reflection shows one ought not to speak roughly about the phenomenon in order to master it), one may simply note that the share of national income going to wages has significantly increased in the seventies and decreased recently, the exact timing varying from one country to another. Some economists argue that the increase was, after some lag, responsible for a significant part of unemployment growth; other economists disagree. Clearly the former now expect to see a stronger curbing of unemployment trends than is forecast by the latter. Precise econometric inference about the direct and indirect impacts of labour costs on the concomitant and subsequent demands for labour by firms is, in this case, inescapable. The case is of course not special.

One cannot, however, entertain the hope that one will ever precisely know all determinants of socio-economic phenomena.

Some trend changes will be neither forecast nor explained, even ex post. Early detection of these trend changes reduces forecasting errors. In this respect purely statistical methods of time-series analysis have a major role to play. Indeed, the whole field of seasonal adjustment techniques may be seen as aiming at detection of trend changes in short-term evolutions. One must also refer to the useful techniques proposed by Brown et al. (1975) for detecting not only trend changes but also other regression coefficient changes.

Similarly, the search for leading indicators within a set of available related time series may be viewed as a purely statistical problem. But it also happens that the most significant information results from a deeper subject-matter analysis, often assisted by statistical inference. In the study of business fluctuations, there is a long tradition of concern for leading indicators, which were the basis for the 'Harvard barometer' in the thirties. Most of the work did not use rigorous statistical inference and rather attempted to be broad, both as to the number of variables and as to the diversity of historical periods; it showed that a great many patterns can be observed, with, however, some tendency for some variables often to change earlier than others (Zarnowitz, 1985). On more limited data sets formalized procedures intended to detect Granger causal orderings between time series are more and more often applied, showing for instance that, on the quarterly US data from 1949 to 1983, movements of the real interest rate lead those of the nominal interest rate, the quantity of money, the price level and industrial production (Litterman and Weiss, 1985).

But even detection of unexplained trend changes may also benefit from a particular scrutiny of the subject matter. For instance, the most uncertain hypothesis to be made for demographic projections may very well be the one concerning future fertility. Everything contributing to an improvement of our knowledge of human fertility may then be valuable.[6] (This might indeed be one of the outcomes of the ISI World Fertility Survey.) In the particular case of French fertility, knowledge of the downturn that occurred in about 1965 has somewhat improved as a result of careful studies made since then. Completed families reached their maximum number of children for the generation of mothers born between 1930 and 1934; but this

---

[6] This seems to be the main message conveyed by the four papers on fertility prospects in United Nations (1979).

timing applying for the French population as a whole has to be advanced by fifteen years for women belonging to the higher social groups or having received a university education, the maximum then concerning the generation born between 1915 and 1919 (INSEE, 1984). One also notes that delay between marriage and the first child increased after 1975 for the whole French population but since the early sixties for women with a university education (Desplanques and de Saboulin, 1986). In other words the 1965 downturn was announced (but not noticed) in 1950 by the behaviour of the higher social groups. This suggests that particular observation of these groups, if it can be made precise, may be valuable.

4. Formalized statistical projections

The preceding sections exhibit the great variety of investigations and operations that occur in the process of preparing socio-economic projections. Focusing on fully formalized procedures is, however, advisable for a closer examination of some methodological issues. One may moreover hope that actual use of these procedures will progressively increase as knowledge of socio-economic phenomena improves and rigour in projection practices increases.

The main methodological issues then are those concerning the choice of the model within which formalized procedures with good statistical properties will be defined. When one wants to project a particular variable of interest, three main questions have to be answered at the modelling stage.

(i)   Which other variables have to be simultaneously considered? One knows that interdependencies exist and that taking them into account may result in higher accuracy. Usually one even has definite prior beliefs about the list of related variables. Which of them should be present in the model?

(ii) Which variables ought to be treated as exogenous and as the object of an independent projection? Indeed, when causality only runs from x to y with no feedback and when x is easy to forecast, projection of x may usefully be taken as given for the projection of y. Even when forecast of x is difficult, one may want to make explicit assumptions about it rather than to treat it as responsible only for random stationary perturbations.

(iii)   Which restrictions have to be incorporated from the beginning into the structure of the model? Prior knowledge of the
phenomenon may be more or less specific and imply more or
less precise consequences on the system of relationship
between the variables.

When asked to answer the three preceding questions, experts
vary in their attitude. I may call two typical attitudes respectively
'empiricist' and 'rationalist'. The empiricist has a systematic distrust
of prior ideas, whether they come from a subject matter theory or
from anywhere else; he often claims that 'the data should speak for
themselves'. The rationalist has the opposite view and expresses
contempt about 'measurement without theory'.[7] The empiricist
does not see why he should bother considering a large number of
variables simultaneously; he does not expect to gain significantly in
forecasting accuracy by making dubious exogenous projections on
supposedly related series; his model is as little specific as possible
while having the fundamental simplicity required for transparency.
The rationalist has his theory and imposes it, with all its particularities, on the model 'even when the data is telling one to reject the
theory';[8] he often wants to deal with many variables, within a
system of equations with quite specific forms and is ready to rely on
a number of exogenous projections. The empiricist is a Box–Jenkins
adept; the rationalist needs so much computation on his model that
he has little care for statistical estimation and is usually unable to
give any measure about the accuracy of his projection.

Of course, the above picture is a caricature, but it should reflect
a real opposition that the history of econometrics illustrates.[9]
During the interwar period the empiricist attitude prevailed for the
study of macroeconomic phenomena, leading for instance to the
ambitious programme of the National Bureau of Economic
Research (Burns and Mitchell, 1946) and, with a more methodological purpose, to two Cowles Commission books (Tintner, 1940;
Davis, 1941). But as a result of a major reflection and research
effort at the same Cowles Commission during and immediately

---

[7] 'A sample of observations is just a set of cold, uninteresting numbers unless we
have a theory concerning the stochastic mechanism that has produced them',
T. Haavelmo, p. 265, in Koopmans (1950).

[8] C. Granger, p. 151 in the discussion of Hendry and Richard (1983).

[9] But econometrics is not special in this respect. See for instance R.D. Lee, 'New
methods for forecasting fertility: an overview' in United Nations (1979).

after the war,[10] a methodology stressing the role of theoretical specification emerged. This methodology dominated econometrics and led to what was called here (in section 1) the second method for macroeconomic projections. Recently, however, it was realized that this domination was perhaps too one-sided. The doubts gave rise to what was called here the third method. Looking at the actual performances of alternative methods of macroeconomic forecasting, one now realizes that, if the second method is indeed the most appropriate for projections extending one year or more into the future, for shorter horizons a purely empiricist approach may be better.[11]

More generally, agreement progressively emerges on the view that the best attitude should be in the middle range between the empiricist and the rationalist positions: a good theory, when it exists, improves projections and should be incorporated in the model; but since specifications often have to be more precise than is warranted by the theory, statistical testing should be performed and preference should be given to robustness against sophistication.

When this is accepted, a question, however, remains as to what should be particularly stressed in the specification of the model: the structural interdependencies or the dynamic pattern? Econometricians tend to give first consideration to the former, time-series analysts to the latter.[12] Indeed, it may be more generally true that subject matter theories provide a reliable guide for the choice of the variables to be simultaneously considered and for the specification of the main factors that directly determine each variable, but that these theories say very little about the time profiles resulting from a number of lags. It then falls to statistical inference to decide, the rule for the modelling stage being to avoid unduly constraining the dynamic specification. Emphasis should moreover differ, depending on the length of the intended horizon; the time

---

[10] The best reference to the discussions that occurred at the time is the exchange between Koopmans and Vining, which was reprinted in Gordon and Klein (1966).

[11] This is the conclusion drawn of the very extensive recent survey appearing in Fildes (1985).

[12] Of course, neither of the two groups completely ignores the other dimension. Econometricians in particular are, and have always been, aware of the time aspect; the famous Cowles Commission monograph 10 was entitled *Statistical Inference in Dynamic Economic Models* (Koopmans, 1950).

structure is likely to be particularly important for short-term projections, interdependencies for longer-term ones.

5. Some philosophical issues

The International Statistical Institute recently adopted a code of ethics. This code is silent about whether or how statisticians ought to make projections. Would it be that this activity raises no ethical problem? Certainly not. At the end of this talk, I cannot neglect considering the various issues involved.

The first one is to know whether making projections is compatible with the requirements for objectivity to which statisticians should adhere, official statisticians still more rigorously than others. When I was a young statistician, some older ones indeed claimed there was no compatibility. Although this extreme stand is no longer often heard, we must be clear on why we now consider it unjustified.

Fundamentally it is because there is a need for objective projections and because statisticians are better prepared than others to make them. Projections are motivated by a concern; they are needed for answering relevant questions about the future, in the same way as observations are needed to answer relevant questions about the present. They are intended to improve control of human destinies, and this requires that they later be as accurate as is feasible.

I shall submit that objectivity of projections implies fulfilment of two conditions. In the first place, the concepts used must be objective and this has precisely the same meaning as to say that statistical concepts must be objective: whereas a concept is always a construct, this construct must aim at being as adequate as possible to the questions it concerns and be as well-understood commonly as possible.[13] In the second place, projections must use as effectively as possible the existing objective knowledge about the phenomenon, this knowledge consisting of both a theory, dealing with the phenomenon in general, and data, concerning the particular case.

If statisticians have been disturbed by making projections, it is precisely because of the second requirement. Disputes or doubts

---

[13] From this point of view it may be instructive to reflect on whether it is ethically sound for French statisticians to issue projections of the foreign population living in France whereas the real concern has more to do with the race composition of the population, but this is not made explicit.

may indeed occur both on what is existing objective knowledge and on what is its best possible use. But the range of the disputes and their impact may be minimized by what might be called objective behaviour, a behaviour that statisticians have other occasions to follow. The theory incorporated in existing knowledge ought to be commonly accepted, as an acceptable approximation, by knowledgeable people. This consideration recommends that badly understood phenomena be the subject of pure assumptions, which then have to be made explicit. Use of existing knowledge should not be intentionally biased and should be competently done. The preceding sections show that such rules of behaviour do not fully erase all difficulties but they greatly reduce them.

Finally, since projections will nevertheless have a lower degree of objectivity than do corresponding statistics, multiplicity is advisable. It is feasible since projections need far smaller resources than the collection of statistics. It can be achieved by the use of several alternative sets of assumptions on the most crucial and debatable factors, such as fertility trends in demographic projections or the determinants of investment in medium-term macroeconomic projections. It is also better achieved if two or several teams of competent people simultaneously make projections about the same phenomenon. Transparency and objectivity may moreover be served by the practice, sometimes applied in France and reported in section 1, according to which the main exogenous hypotheses are chosen by an independent body, which is distinct from the institution producing the projections.

Ethical questions also concern the diffusion given to projections. It happens indeed that objectivity is lost along the channels of transmission of information to the general public: attention is then focused on results that may appear as sensational and one often forgets to mention the exact meaning of these results. But it should be noted that the same kind of distortion sometimes occurs in the diffusion of statistics or of many scientific results. In this respect the rules of behaviour to be given to projectionists do not differ from those that statisticians, and more generally scientists, ought to follow.

References

P. Artus, M. Deleau and P. Malgrange (1986), *Modélisation macro-économique*, Economica, Paris.

C. Bianchi, J.-L. Brillet and G. Calzolari (1984), 'Analyse et mesure de l'incertitude d'un modèle économétrique. Application au modèle Mini-DMS', *Annales de l'INSEE*, 54.

G. Box and G. Jenkins (1970), *Time Series Analysis, Forecasting and Control*, Holden Day, San Francisco.

R.L. Brown, J. Durbin and M. Evans (1975), 'Techniques for testing the constancy of regression relationship over time', *Journal of the Royal Statistical Society*, Ser. B, 37(2).

A. Burns and W. Mitchell (1946), *Measuring Business Cycles*, National Bureau of Economic Research, New York.

H. Davis (1941), *The Analysis of Economic Times Series*, Bloomington Press, Bloomington, IN.

G. Desplanques and M. de Saboulin (1986), 'Mariage et premier enfant: un lien qui se défait', *Economie et Statistique*, 193.

T. Doan, R. Litterman and C. Sims (1984), 'Forecasting and conditional projection using realistic prior distributions', *Econometric Review*, 3(1).

R. Fair (1984), *Specification, Estimation and Analysis of Macroeconometric Models*, Harvard University Press, Cambridge, MA.

R. Fildes (1985), 'Quantitative forecasting – the state of the art: econometric models', *Journal of the Operation Research Society*, July.

D. Fouquet, J.-M. Charpin, H. Guillaume, P.-A. Muet and D. Vallet (1978), 'DMS, Modèle dynamique multi-sectoriel', *Collections de l'INSEE*, Ser. C, 64–5.

R. Gordon and L. Klein (1966), *Readings in Business Cycles*, George Allen & Unwin, London.

H. Guillaume and P.-A. Muet (1979), 'Simulations et multiplicateurs du modèle DMS', *Revue économique*, 30, pp. 207–43.

D. Hendry and J. Richard (1983), 'The econometric analysis of economic time series', *International Statistical Review*, August.

INSEE (1984), 'La taille des familles et le milieu social', *Premiers résultats*, 23.

M. Intriligator (1978), *Econometric Models, Techniques and Applications*, North Holland, Amsterdam.

T. Koopmans (1950) (ed.), *Statistical Inference in Dynamic Economic Models*, Cowles Commission Monograph 10, Wiley, New York.

J.-C. Labat and J. Dekneudt (1986), 'Projection de la population étrangère résidant en France métropolitaine', *Archives et documents*, 166, INSEE, Paris.

R. Litterman and L. Weiss (1985), 'Money, real interest rates and output: a reinterpretation of postwar US data', *Econometrica*, 53, pp. 129–56.

OECD (1986), *Economic Outlook*, 39, Paris.

C. Sims (1980), 'Macroeconomics and reality', *Econometrica*, 48, pp. 1–48.

N. Tabard (1985), 'Structure économique des communes, reproduction, consommation', *Consommation*, 1.

G. Tintner (1940), *The Variate Difference Method*, Bloomington Press, Bloomington, IN.

United Nations (1979), 'Prospects of population: methodology and assumptions', Papers of an ad hoc group of experts on demographic projections, *Population Studies* 67, UN, New York.

(1980), 'Patterns of urban and rural population growth', *Population Studies* 68, UN, New York.

(1985), 'World population prospects: estimates and projections as assessed in 1982', *Population Studies* 86, UN, New York.

V. Zarnowitz (1985), 'Recent work on business cycles in historical perspective', *Journal of Economic Literature*, 23(2).

4

Diagnosing unemployment trends

In order to give a more concrete content to the considerations of chapter 1 and to complement them, it is necessary to select one particular subject on which one will follow the various operations through which diagnoses are eventually formed. Unemployment is obviously the subject to be selected on this occasion: it is the most acute macroeconomic problem in our European countries during this long period that started fifteen years ago and is not yet over. I have spent a good deal of my time on the subject over these past years; above all Professor Federico Caffè frequently expressed his concern about it and considered it one of the main reasons why economists had to advise governments.

Clearly diagnosing unemployment trends is difficult. The origins of the various uncertainties will clearly appear, I hope, in what follows. So much so that my presentation may even convey a distressing feeling: the difficulties might be taken as opposing an insuperable obstacle to attempts at diagnosis. In order to avoid this misunderstanding, to which many independent published statements give credit nowadays, I think it is necessary to state, right at the beginning of this lecture, that the past record is not as bad as some people say. I do not know of any systematic confrontation of the diagnoses given during the past two decades with what was later observed; but I think I know the situation well enough to give my own testimony with confidence.

It is certainly true that, around 1970, most European economists anticipated that fast growth and full employment would go on for many years, although some had already pointed out that the Bretton Woods international system was breaking apart and that this was bound to disrupt the prevailing orderly growth. But by the

Second Caffè Lecture 1990.

middle of the 1970s optimism had disappeared much more quickly among economists working on macroeconomic diagnosis than among many other groups (in France among politicians, business-men, trade unions, etc.). Medium-term projections in particular, which then appeared as shocking, showed that the demand for labour was very likely to grow much less quickly than the supply of labour (in Malinvaud, 1984, p. 111 I referred to some published projections of the time). Similarly, in contradiction to what is often said now, the 1987 upturn in investment was forecast in medium-term projections made in France in 1986 (see DMS, 1987). The error in these medium-term diagnoses was mainly that they under-estimated the importance of the shifts: the slowdown in the late 1970s and early 1980s, the more recent upturn; but such an underestimation is understandable considering the uncertainty of the diagnosis.

Short-term assessments of course made a number of mistakes, the most noticeable one having been to join the then prevailing wave of pessimism during about ten weeks after the October 1987 stock market crash: growth rates peaked in 1988 and were still above trend in 1989. But as a whole over the past two decades they were more often right than wrong in announcing subsequent economic evolution, the record being no worse, it seems to me, than it had been in the 1960s. Short-term forecast of the trend in the number of unemployed people was on several occasions erroneous, but mainly because public authorities chose in the meantime active labour-market policies whose first impact was to curb the increase in unemployment without really changing macroeconomic conditions.

The correct evaluation is thus not that diagnosis is doomed to failure but rather that it faces difficulties; those are serious enough to react negatively on the reliability of what is announced. Improve-ments are certainly feasible, although they will in any case leave large uncertainty margins; they are moreover likely to require often tedious and piecemeal investigation.

In this lecture I shall consider in turn the various aspects of the work devoted to unemployment diagnosis. Hopefully progress could be made on each of these aspects, resulting in an overall accuracy improvement. The first aspect will concern conceptuali-zation of the main categories that we use for our assessments. The second will be analysis of workers' behaviour both as supplying labour and as being involved in more or less-important search activities. The third will be the study of the mismatch between the compositions of, respectively, the supply of labour and the demand for it, more particularly the composition by skills. The fourth will assume the greatest importance since it will concern the demand for labour.

1. The main analytical categories

According to a simplistic idea, assessments about the course of unemployment would directly follow from assessments about the course of the demand for labour, because unemployment would exactly match the excess of a rather rigid supply of labour over the demand for it. The idea is not wholly misleading and I shall indeed stress here the strategic role of the demand for labour for the diagnoses on unemployment. However, the picture is not as simple as that. Some significant factors act on unemployment independently of any action on the demand for labour, or beyond any such action; they may concern the supply of labour, but they may also concern the process of matching between supply and demand on the labour market.

(i) In order to sort out the effects of the various factors, depending on the way in which they act, analysts often proposed to decompose unemployment into additive components. It turns out that many proposals in this direction are more confusing than really useful. Indeed, introducing an additive decomposition is tantamount to assuming a particular form of the relationship combining the effects of the various factors, and in many cases an additive form is not appropriate. This is why I think we ought to stick to a decomposition into only two parts, frictional unemployment and disequilibrium unemployment.

The distinction between these two parts is related to exact definitions chosen for the supply of labour and the demand for it. Indeed, formally let the supply be S and the demand D, disequilibrium unemployment U_d is by definition the difference between the two:

$$U_d = S - D. \tag{1}$$

Frictional unemployment U_f is the rest of unemployment U:

$$U = U_d + U_f. \tag{2}$$

Unemployment has been defined by labour statisticians as being the difference between the labour force N and employment L:

$$U = N - L. \tag{3}$$

(ii) Employment is of course related to supply and demand. A perfect matching on the labour market would imply:

$$L = \text{Min}\{S, D\}. \tag{4}$$

As soon as supply exceeds demand, unfortunately the normal case nowadays, employment would be equal to demand. Equations (1), (2) and (3) would then imply:

$$N = S + U_f. \tag{5}$$

One would distinguish in the labour force two parts, exactly as one distinguishes two components of unemployment. The first part would be really available for work; this would be the supply of labour. Frictional unemployment would then correspond to the fact that part of the labour force is normally busy in the process of searching for jobs. The adverb 'normally' here is important; it refers of course to normal conditions of equilibrium between supply and demand on the labour market. More generally let us denote this part of labour force that is not really available for work by R:

$$N = S + R. \tag{6}$$

Exact matching between supplies and demands on the labour market would imply $U_f = R$, i.e. that frictional unemployment be explained only by normal search for work. Of course this search could increase or decrease; it would do so for other reasons than the labour market disequilibrium, for instance because of changes in the perceived urgency of the need to earn a labour income.

But one cannot expect a perfect match on the labour market. The compositions of supply and demand differ, particularly with respect to locations requested and to qualifications. The determination of employment as a function of supply and demand depends on the degree of mismatch, which I assume to be characterized by an indicator m:

$$L = f(S, D; m) < \text{Min} \{S, D\}. \tag{7}$$

Even in case of excess supply, employment is lower than demand. But it is natural to assume that f is homogeneous of degree 1 in S and D and that the difference between demand and employment is all the smaller as excess supply is more important (and as mismatch m is smaller). Homogeneity means that the positive derivatives f'_S and f'_D are smaller than 1; f'_m is negative. Here is for instance a formula that has this property and was used in this context:

$$L = [S^{-\rho} + D^{-\rho}]^{-1/\rho} \tag{8}$$

where ρ is a positive number which is a decreasing function of m (as ρ increases indefinitely L tends to the minimum of S and D). With (7) replacing (4), equations (1), (2), (3) and (6) imply:

$$U_f = R + D - L. \tag{9}$$

Frictional unemployment is due both to normal search and to the effect of the mismatch between the supply of labour and the demand for it.

(iii) Clearly the decomposition of the labour force into S and R, or equivalently the exact definition of the supply of labour, is conventional since a convention has to be chosen in order to define what is considered as normal search by workers. One easily understands that a similar problem concerns the exact definition of the demand for labour. Let J be the total number of jobs available. Vacancies V are given by the excess of J over L:

$$V = J - L, \tag{10}$$

an equation that is similar to (3). Labour demand has not to be considered as equal to J, because employers too are normally searching for appropriate candidates that will fill a vacant job. In parallel with equation (6) one may write:

$$J = D + Q \tag{11}$$

Q being that part of available jobs which, because of employers' search, would be vacant under normal conditions on the labour market. One easily thinks of reasons that may explain changes in Q; for instance if dismissals are made easier by a relaxation of a labour law, appointments will appear less irreversible and some employers will become less wary when recruiting, Q will correspondingly decrease.

(iv) It has been observed, since the 1930s at least, that unemployment U and vacancies V tended to move in opposite directions, with U increasing and V decreasing during depressions. Considering the rates of unemployment ($u = U/N$) and vacancies (v usually measured as V/L but more conveniently defined as V/N), the name 'Beveridge curve' has been given to the plot that successive observations would trace on the (u,v) plane if normal search activities and mismatch between supply and demand did not change. This relationship is precisely implied by equation (7) ruling the determination of employment. Indeed, taking (3), (6), (10) and (11) into account we may write (7) as:

$$N - U = f(N - R, N - U + V - Q; m). \tag{12}$$

The homogeneity of f also permits us to write:

$$1 - u = f(1 - r, 1 - u + v - q; m) \tag{13}$$

where r and q are rates of normal search (R/N and Q/N) by workers and employers. The type of relation implied by this equation appears more clearly if we differentiate it:

$$dv = -\frac{1 - f'_D}{f'_D} \, du + dq + \frac{f'_s}{f'_D} \, dr - \frac{f'_m}{f'_D} \, dm. \tag{14}$$

The vacancy rate is a decreasing function of the unemployment rate when q, r and m are held constant; this relation is precisely traced by the Beveridge curve (figure 4.1).[1]

But this curve may shift because of changes in normal search activities and in the mismatch between the structures of demands and supplies. Equation (14) shows that the curve shifts to the right

---

[1] The existence of an inverse statistical relationship between the unemployment rate and the vacancy rate was first noted by W. Beveridge (1944). The name 'Beveridge curve' has been adopted for fits of this relationship or for its formal rationalizations. The Beveridge curve is derived here from the function that was assumed to determine employment, given labour supply and demand. But the opposite case could have been made. Indeed the Beveridge curve can be rationalized as an equilibrium relation when one considers flows on the labour market, an approach that is particularly suited for the analysis of search activities (see chapter 5).

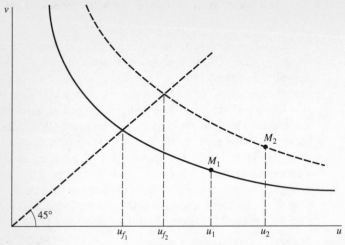

Figure 4.1

(v increases for a given u) if search tends to increase or if the degree of mismatch increases (f'_m is negative).

   (v) I shall not insist here on the conventions that are commonly used for the exact measures of the various concepts just presented, from the statistical ones (labour force, employment and unemployment) to those introduced for economic analysis, like frictional unemployment. I have discussed them in a little more detail on other occasions (for instance in Malinvaud, 1984 and 1988). I shall just mention that more and more often economists tend to use the Beveridge curve for their definition of the frictional rate of unemployment u_f: according to a simple convention this rate is given by the point where the curve intersects the bissectrice (see figure 4.1). This definition leads to the equation:

$$1 - u_f = f(1 - r, 1 - q; m) \tag{15}$$

which results from (13) and well shows how the rate in question depends on normal search activities and on the degree of mismatch. A movement on the curve from one period to another then signals a change in the rate of disequilibrium unemployment $u_d = u - u_f$, whereas a shift of the curve signals a change in the rate of frictional unemployment. The actual increase from u_1 to u_2, say, is then decomposed into two parts $u_{d_2} - u_{d_1}$ and $u_{f_2} - u_{f_1}$. Identification of the positions of the Beveridge curve in each period is the only requirement for the decomposition to be feasible (the requirement, that I shall not discuss here, is in practice more severe than one would wish, both because of lack of reliable data on vacancies and econometric identification difficulties).

The interest of these various definitions is to distinguish between different groups of factors that act on unemployment and explain its changes; different groups that have to be individually studied, in particular for a good diagnosis about current evolution. Referring to equations (1), (2) and (15) we shall consider in section 2 the behaviour of individuals, which determines the supply of labour and normal search activity (one of the three determinants of frictional unemployment). Section 3 will be devoted to the measure and role of the mismatch (another determinant of frictional unemployment). Section 4 will concern the behaviour of enterprises in their demand for labour in the short and medium run. The normal search activity of firms (Q) will not be discussed because I should have very little to say about it. This aspect of the problem was neglected in the research of the past twenty years, which on the contrary dealt with all the other aspects that I am going to consider.

I shall not of course present a full survey of each topic. My intention is rather to take a bird's eye view of all of them so that the conditions under which unemployment diagnosis actually operates clearly appear.

2. Labour supply and search behaviour

Three main themes have been the focus of attention by those in charge of forecasting individual behaviour with respect to the labour market: How is the participation of women in the labour force likely to evolve? How sensitive is the supply of labour with respect to the real wage rate? Is there an increase in the worker's propensity to extend search time before taking a job, and if so why? Let us consider these three questions in turn.

(i) In many countries there was a surprisingly rapid increase in female participation during the 1970s and 1980s, unfortunately at the time when a depression in labour markets developed. In France for instance the demographic projections, using methods of extrapolation of previously observed trends, had anticipated an increase, but not the very rapid one that occurred. The phenomenon is not yet well understood and the reasons for the present large intercountry disparities remain somewhat obscure (in 1986 the rate of participation of women aged 15 to 64 ranged in the EEC from 34 per cent in Spain to 78 per cent in Denmark, according to 'The labour market in the Community', *European Economy*, 38, 1988).

Many econometric studies were made about the labour supply of women, using samples of individual data (see for instance chapter 2 in Ashenfelter and Layard, 1985); they showed in particular the importance at any time of the education and family status of women. But they do not suffice for the explanation of what is observed. For instance the decrease in the fertility rate can only explain a small part of the phenomenon. One suspects a role was played by a number of factors such as a greater availability of part-time jobs or even the increase in unemployment, against the risk of which a second wage-earner in the family offers some protection; but again each of these factors cannot have had more than a small impact. Certainly social attitudes and norms matter, but one does not know how to find for them independent characterizations that could be helpful in forecasting. In these circumstances detailed and accurate observation of the actual evolution (by age, level of education, family status, etc.) provides the main basis for a forecast, which cannot claim to be more than an intelligent extrapolation.

(ii) The elasticity of the labour supply with respect to the real wage is important for various questions of economic theory. It was a topic attracting particular attention in econometric studies (see for instance chapters 1 and 2 in Ashenfelter and Layard, 1985). For adult men one may safely conclude that the elasticity is negative but quite small in absolute value (around -0.1); this result well agrees with the observation of a long-run slowly decreasing trend in the length of time spent at work as standards of living rise. For women various studies lead to different and imprecise results; the overall conclusion seems to be the existence of a positive and moderate elasticity (between 0.5

and 1.0). Such estimates of course matter when diagnosis has to consider a situation for which a break in the trend of real wage rates is anticipated.

New subtleties were introduced in the study of this relationship when the idea of intertemporal substitutability in labour supply became fashionable in some universities around 1980. The idea was to distinguish between the long-run wage elasticity, which had been earlier considered, and a short-run one that would characterize the effect of real wage changes expected to be temporary; the claim was that this short-run elasticity might be much higher. If such were the case, the distinction would be important for some applications in diagnosis analysis. It is fair to say, however, that thus far attempts at substantiating the claim of a large short-run elasticity have failed.

(iii) Reaching an objective assessment about possible changes in the intensity of search by unemployed workers has been recognized for some time to be important. It was so first in order to dispose of the argument that was occasionally heard in the 1970s when unemployment started growing quickly: some people were then saying that the explanation was an increased reluctance of unemployed workers to take available jobs. Although extreme assertions of this type are no longer much heard, it remains useful to know which part, if any, in the rise of unemployment could be so explained and therefore could persist even when the demand for labour has fully recovered. The question also raises valuable policy issues: to the extent that a change in workers' attitudes may be due to a change in labour regulation or labour protection, there may be a tradeoff between employment and other social objectives; taking this tradeoff into account is then required for good policy advising.

One may think of quite a few factors that might have caused an increase in the normal duration of job search. Before I say a few things about some of them, I must point out that the end of job search is not always accepting employment but may also be giving up, i.e. stopping search and so dropping out of the labour force. With respect to equation (6) factors explaining a decrease in normal search R should not be considered as implying only an increase in labour supply S but often also a decrease in labour force N as recorded in the statistics. This is why it was sometimes suggested that labour market analysis take a broader definition of the labour force than the one adopted by statisticians, and add to the latter an estimate of the number of 'discouraged workers'. But the suggestion is not really workable because it would make the line between being in or out of the labour force still more fuzzy than it already is. One must simply recognize a difficulty with the application of the formal apparatus presented in the preceding section and remember that factors acting positively on R may also act positively on N.

The remark must go still further, because the disequilibrium of the labour market, i.e. U_d, also acts on the labour force: a decrease in labour demand, which implies a decrease in the number of available jobs and an increase in disequilibrium unemployment, also leads to an increase in the number of discouraged workers and to a decrease in the labour force. For econometric applications of the equations of the preceding section the correct solution is to consider this feedback from the labour market disequilibrium to the labour force N as being a feedback to labour supply S rather than to normal search R, which has been defined as independent of market disequilibrium; in other words, S should be recognized as being somewhat also a function of D.

About normal search one noted that its length systematically varies with demographic characteristics, increasing with age and being somewhat longer for women than for men. A change in the demographic composition of the labour force may then entail a change of the aggregate amount of normal search. But calculations show that the contribution of this factor to the increase in European unemployment was negligible.

The impacts of some of the potential factors are much more difficult to gauge. For instance it is natural to suspect that increase in real incomes permits people to be less eager to find a job quickly than they were twenty years ago. Similarly, particularities and imperfections of European housing markets, together with the increase in the share of owner-occupied dwellings, contributes to explain a low geographical mobility of workers and may even be responsible for some decrease in this mobility, hence an increase in normal job-search time. However, the effect of such slow changes in economic conditions can be evaluated only by reference to differences observed in cross-sections of individual households and one then wonders how the transposition of synchronic differences to changes through time should be made.

More precise econometric results are now available about the role of unemployment compensation schemes, whether organized as insurance or as assistance. To what extent does better compensation lead to an increase in the duration of unemployment, before either acceptance of a job or withdrawal from the labour force? A full answer would have to distinguish between the many features of actual compensation schemes; these features vary from one country to another and have also varied within each country. For ease of exposition I shall consider here just two main features: the degree of income replacement, i.e. the ratio between the two incomes obtained when respectively unemployed or employed, and the duration of eligibility after the last employment. Both a higher replacement ratio and a longer eligibility duration have been found to lead to longer average unemployment spells. But the influence of the replacement ratio seems to be small (I gave some figures in Malinvaud, 1984; more recent references will be found in chapter 5 here), whereas new results suggest that the eligibility duration is more important and might explain a small but significant part of international differences in unemployment rates (see for instance Jackman et al., 1990). Improvement in unemployment compensation during the 1970s may have increased frictional unemployment somewhat; but this factor should have played no role in the 1980s since there was no improvement, but rather in some cases a small reduction in compensation.

One also suspects that labour market policies may react on normal search time and on unemployment.[2] Some training programmes are well known as having temporarily withdrawn a number of people from unemployment, a feature that short-term unemployment diagnosis must of course take into account. Whether these programmes helped in reducing the time later required for finding a job is more uncertain but cannot be ruled out. Well-informed specialists consider that, in Scandinavian countries and Switzerland, employment exchange offices are much more active than elsewhere and put pressure on the unemployed both to look for

---

[2] The case of the Italian 'Cassa integrazione' is of a different nature since it amounts to maintaining employment status for people who are not actually working for more or less-durable periods.

work and to take suitable job offers, a pressure that can be coupled with denial of benefit.

3. The mismatch

(i) Many causes could induce a change in the mismatch between the structural compositions of labour demand and supply. New technologies appear. Consumption of the various goods and services grow at different rates. International competition favours or hits industries, which have different labour requirements and different locations. Simultaneously populations move. Women, whose share in the labour force increases, do not supply exactly the same mix of services as men do. The diffusion of education leads younger workers to apply for qualified jobs more frequently than their predecessors did. The existence of so many shifts makes diagnosis and long-run forecasting difficult. Indeed, mistaken assessments occasionally occur, for instance as to the future prospects of some professions. We may, incidentally, remember the fears expressed twenty years ago about the plethora of educated people that the fast growth of higher education was supposed to bring.

Economists of course know that spontaneous adaptations take place between the structures of demands and supplies, which ought not to be taken as rigidly given. In particular changes in relative wage rates are likely to occur and to induce adaptations. But this market regulating function does not operate perfectly because in particular wages are not fully flexible. One may even have to take into account changes through time or space in relative wage rigidities.

If forecasting is difficult, ex-post assessment is easier than for some of the factors mentioned earlier. Detailed data exist on the structure of unemployment and employment or the labour force. For an exact measurement of the mismatch it would be preferable to use data on labour supply and demand, or on disequilibrium unemployment and labour demand. But the differences between corresponding alternative concepts are small enough for the results concerning structural mismatch to be rather insensitive to a small inadequacy of definitions, except with respect to two important characteristics about which I shall say more below.

Setting these exceptions aside for the moment, I can record that the degree of structural mismatch does not seem to have changed significantly in Europe, at least during the 1970s and up to the middle of the 1980s. Calculations were made in the various countries, notably at the occasion of coordinated national studies within the 'European unemployment programme' (see Bean et al., 1986). In particular with reference to industrial or geographical breakdowns indicators of the dispersion in labour market conditions showed no trend. Hence frictional unemployment could not have changed because of such mismatch. It is sometimes said that the regional mismatch has increased since the middle of the 1980s, particularly in Italy and the UK. In order to check this hypothesis full calculations ought to be updated. We now turn to the aforementioned exceptions.

(ii) The first exception concerns the breakdown by skill types. One notes that not only have the highest levels of unemployment over the last decade been concentrated among the unskilled, but also that unemployment rates of highly skilled labour have increased little over the past twenty years of strong rise in unemployment. One may wonder, however, whether this observation reveals a true increase in the skill mismatch, an increase that would persist even if the labour market overall disequilibrium disappeared. In the first place, skilled labour is, more often than unskilled, a fixed factor of production with a technical ability that is very specific to the products of the firm employing it; hence labour hoarding is particularly important. But this fact cannot have played a notable role in the point at issue because of the sheer length of the period considered and because of labour turnover, which the familiar study of stocks rather than flows on the labour market often tends to underestimate.

Much more important may have been the so-called 'ladder effect'. With the increased slack of the labour market skilled workers may have been inclined to apply for less skilled jobs, for which they usually look attractive to potential employers because of a higher expected productivity, especially if and when production will have to adapt to new circumstances. This competition coming from above on the skill ladder further deteriorates the situation at lower levels.

Danthine et al. (1990), however, draw attention to evidence suggesting that a truly increasing qualification mismatch did occur notwithstanding the ladder phenomenon. They point to the fact that the 1980s seem to have witnessed not only a shift of the skill structure of employment but also a reversal of the trend towards a reduction of wage differentials by skill (figures are given for the UK). This suggests that the structure of the demand for labour is probably shifting towards higher qualifications still more quickly than the structure of the supply. Such an hypothesis is consistent with the common view based on the observation of rapid changes in technologies (but similar changes in former times should not be overlooked) and of the emergence of competitors from the Third World for traditional European industries in which employment of unskilled workers was large.

(iii) Mismatch concerns heterogeneity within labour demand and supply. Some causes of heterogeneity are due to the institutions and functioning of the labour market; they may even be magnified by the overall labour market disequilibrium. Such is the case with a feature that is now identified in Europe with labour market segmentation, namely the coexistence of two kinds of labour contracts, which I shall call for short 'permanent jobs' and 'temporary jobs'. It is appropriate to discuss this feature at some length here, because it is usually neglected in the macroeconomic literature. For so doing I shall refer only to France, the country that I know best. The phenomenon there had some specificities, but not to such an extent as to make it untypical of what happened elsewhere within the European Economic Community (see for instance Blanchot, 1990, and the data available at Eurostat).

A normal labour contract would be signed for an indefinite duration and would give the employee access to an open-ended career with the employer. But contracts for a finite duration ('contrats à durée déterminée') have recently become very common also, as well as contracts for interim work, with which they will be grouped here (the phrase 'emplois précaires' is often used in France for covering both of these kinds of temporary jobs[3]). Why do we speak of labour market segmentation when referring to the co-existence of these two types of contracts?

The concept of segmentation was characterized as follows: 'the labour market can be usefully described as consisting of two sectors: a high-wage (primary) sector with good working conditions, stable employment, and substantial return to human capital variables such as education and experience, and a low-wage (secondary) sector with opposite characteristics. Moreover, primary jobs are rationed' (Dickens and Lang, 1988). Of all these various features,[4] only two really seem to matter for the present European usage, namely that permanent (primary) jobs provide stable employment and are rationed. The other aspects appear as secondary or even as non-existent; for instance speaking of two sectors would be misleading since the same task is often performed side by side by two workers, one holding a permanent contract, the other a temporary one. Since the first of the two relevant features really belongs to the definition, differential rationing between permanent and temporary jobs is the only point that deserves attention at this stage.

Proof of such rationing is provided by the high proportion of workers holding a temporary job and looking for a permanent one: in France in March 1986, it amounted to 32 per cent, out of 34 per cent looking for another job and in comparison with only 6 per cent of the whole employed labour force looking for another job. Among those holding a temporary job and looking for another job, only 10 per cent reported as their main motivation to find better pay, a higher qualification or better working conditions (Heller, 1986). It is pretty clear that most workers holding a temporary job do so for want of having found a permanent one.

This is particularly apparent also in the results of a special survey of people belonging to the 16–26 age group (Glaude and Jarousse, 1988). Among those having a real job (excluding employment in training schemes) 13 per cent thought it was impossible for them to be kept more than a year by their present employer; only for 3 per cent was this situation well accepted; 3 per cent would have left right away if they had found a job corresponding to their wishes; 6 per

[3] Sometimes, but not here, 'temporary jobs' are also meant to include employment in various training schemes created by labour market policies.
[4] In some presentations of the labour market duality it is also specified that the primary sector is unionized, a feature that plays no role in the case under discussion.

cent would have liked to stay for more than a year (4 per cent permanently); 1 per cent did not know.

It may also be significant to note, in particular with respect to current notions about labour market segmentation, that, other things being equal, temporary jobs are somewhat lower-paid than permanent ones: some 10 per cent less according to an econometric study that controlled for a large number of other factors (Elbaum, 1988).

Does the composition of the population holding temporary jobs reveal anything significant, as for the mismatch between labour supply and demand, or incidentally as for discrimination? At first sight the picture may seem similar to the one given by the composition of unemployment; but there are notable differences. 'Rates of temporary employment' (number of workers holding a temporary job over number of wage and salary earners) do not exhibit quite the same pattern as the one provided by unemployment rates; gender disparities disappear: in 1987 the rates were 3.3 per cent for both women and men (unemployment rates being 13.4 and 8.6 per cent respectively); on the contrary disparities by level of qualification are more pronounced, with very few temporary contracts for professionals. Young people are, of course, particularly numerous in holding temporary jobs: the rate was 12.1 per cent in 1987 for the 15–24 age group (the corresponding unemployment rate being 22 per cent). The phenomenon is particularly apparent among the young new entrants into employment: 48 per cent enter with a permanent job (70 per cent for those with an academic education), 26 per cent with a temporary job and 26 per cent with employment in a training scheme (Elbaum, 1988).

It was sometimes said in France that this kind of segmentation meant that an important part of the labour force no longer had access to permanent jobs and was trapped into a life of alternating spells of unemployment and temporary employment. Such is undoubtedly the case for a small group of people with poor employment records; but it is not representative of those holding temporary jobs at any point in time. Among the latter, observed a year later, 8 per cent had dropped out of the labour force, 19 per cent were unemployed (as against 10 per cent for the whole French labour force), 4 per cent were employed in a training programme, 25 per cent were again holding a temporary job and 44 per cent a permanent job (Cézard and Heller, 1988). These data are more consistent with the view that, in many cases, temporary contracts are offered as for a trial period and that having accepted one brings little stigma.

Although the data sources are not as complete as one might wish, it is pretty clear that the importance of temporary jobs grew much in line with unemployment during the 1970s and early 1980s. The longest available series in France does not concern temporary jobs exactly but the proportion of the employed labour force looking for another job because the present one has been taken while waiting for another appropriate opportunity (my translation of 'l'emploi actuel est un emploi d'attente'): the rate was as low as 0.3 or 0.2 per cent in the sixties; it reached 0.9 per cent in 1982 and 1.5 per cent in 1986; it later declined (Thélot, 1985; Cézard and Heller, 1988). Since 1975 we know the number of people who became unemployed because their temporary job (extensive definition) ended: as a ratio of total unemployment, this number more than doubled between 1975 and 1982; later it remained roughly stable (Thélot, 1985). Better series exist for the 1980s; they show that, for the business sector, the rate of temporary employment was equal to roughly 3 per cent in early 1982 (with an unemployment rate of 7.8 per cent) and to 5 per cent when the unemployment rate reached its maximum in 1987 (10.7 per cent); the rate of temporary employment still increased to 6 per cent in 1989; recently it declined to 5.5 per cent while the unemployment rate, stabilized at 9 per cent in 1990, was beginning to increase again.

Neglecting small differences in timing, which may often be explained otherwise, we may view the development of temporary jobs as being to a large extent a consequence of the overall slackness of the labour market. When this slackness increases, workers searching for jobs reduce their claims and become more ready to accept temporary jobs; employers take advantage of the opportunity and save on the fixed costs that permanent recruitment would entail; they are all the more induced to do so as the poor business prospects make them particularly sensitive to uncertainties and therefore less eager to ensure long-term attachment of new employees. This explanation adds a new dimension to the rationing that aggregate unemployment reveals. There is not only a shortage of available jobs; the composition of these jobs is also distorted toward short durations, whereas most workers are looking for permanent employment.

Taking this new dimension into account, let us come back to the categories proposed in the first section. We then have to distinguish between those changes in segmentation that are induced by the varying degree of overall market disequilibrium and those that may be due to more permanent changes in institutions and practices. The latter ones imply changes in the normal search component R of the labour force; hence in frictional unemployment. Indeed, an increasing segmentation imposes on workers a more frequent exposure to job changes, hence to job search; it also implies a longer search time because, before accepting a temporary job, most workers want to test whether they could not obtain a permanent one. On the other hand, it would be inappropriate in our framework to withdraw from the labour supply S what is the result of the changing mismatch and search following from those changes in segmentation that are induced by variations in labour market slackness.

Incidentally it is worth noting here that this study reveals the interest that would attach to a more systematic study of flows on the labour market than is now current. This interest will appear again in chapter 5. Considering national accounts in the first chapter I stressed that the data bases on wealth and productive stocks were underdeveloped with respect to the data on flows; correspondingly macroeconomic analysis of the supply of goods and demand for them tend to pay relatively too much attention to flows and too little to stocks. The situation is precisely the reverse for the analysis of the labour market.

4. The demand for labour

By far the most strategic factor in unemployment diagnosis is commonly the demand for labour by firms. But this demand is a complex phenomenon whose many determinants are more or less interdependent and act more or less upstream of observed facts. To analyse it requires the study of the full macroeconomic situation. Indeed, this is why unemployment diagnosis requires a collaboration between labour economists and macroeconomists, the first ones being particularly knowledgeable about many specific institutional features of the labour market, which matter most for frictional unemployment, whereas the second ones are used to consider market disequilibria and their interdependence.

Since analysis of the demand for labour has to be embedded in a full-fledged macroeconomic analysis it may involve a wide range of economic relations. For this purpose experts often put to work their macroeconometric models with large numbers of equations, most of which matter directly or indirectly for the demand for labour. But in order usefully to reflect on this occasion, we must take an overview of the subject and limit attention to the proximate and most important causes.

(i) We may first concentrate on the two main direct determinants: the demand for goods that is addressed to firms and the wage rate. Hardly anybody dismisses the idea that these two determinants are relevant; but there is still today some confusion about the way in which they ought to enter into a correct diagnosis. I may, then, be excused for going back to basics.

Let me start from a simple but somewhat dangerous graph. At each level of the demand for goods there would be an inverse relation between the demand for labour and the wage rate. A decrease in the wage would lead to an increase in employment along the curve; an increase in the demand for goods would also lead to an increase in employment, the curve moving upward.

The graph is dangerous because one is inclined to consider it as applying to a representative firm and to transpose its conclusions as directly applying at the macroeconomic level also. For the firm the graph makes sense only if, having placed the nominal wage rate as abscissa, one supposes a fixed price of output, or alternatively if one uses as abscissa the real wage rate, defined as the ratio between the nominal wage rate and the output price. The first solution permits a more direct interpretation, but one that has little interest for a macroeconomist since variations in the nominal wage rate always react on prices, most often close to one for one. One must therefore prefer to put the real rate as abscissa.

The transposition to the macroeconomic level is no less risky. The demand for the firm's goods comes from all its clients: other firms and/or individuals, many of them being wage earners. Wage earners spend according to their incomes, which vary with the real wage rate. (There may be some compensation coming from the demand of non-wage earners; but this is likely to be partial only; see chapter 6 and Malinvaud, 1991.) Whatever the microeconomic value of the graph, its macroeconomic transposition cannot be justified if it leads

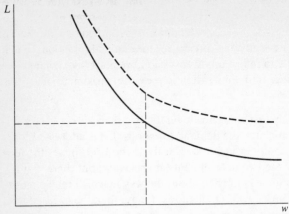

Figure 4.2

one to ignore the dependence of the aggregate demand for goods on the real wage rate.

So, if a graph of this type is to be used for the present purpose, it should be directly specified at the macroeconomic level. This has a consequence for the nature of the argument based on the graph and another consequence for the definition and shape of the demand curve.

The argument admits some autonomy of the real wage determination. It indeed suggests that one first attempts to make a diagnosis about the level and evolution of the real wage, before one makes the diagnosis about the level and evolution of the demand for labour, with of course the possibility of a feedback. The hypothesis of some autonomy does not disturb me, because I believe it is realistic: there is enough rigidity in real wages for it to justify the suggested logical approach as a first step in the analysis, the second step permitting recognition of whatever interdependence was initially neglected. But I must say that some of my economist colleagues are quite reluctant to accept the hypothesis.

As for the curve, it must be defined not for a given level of the aggregate demand for goods, but for given levels of the autonomous factors of this demand, i.e. exclusive of what results from the multiplier phenomenon, particularly as it concerns the income effect of changes in the wage rate. Autonomous demand factors may be the foreign demand for goods and services, the foreign real interest rate, the stance of fiscal and monetary policy. Such a redefinition reacts on the shape of the curve, since an increase in the real wage rate leads to an increase in the aggregate demand for goods, hence to an increase also in the demand for labour by enterprises. This phenomenon runs counter to the supposed downward orientation of the curve; one must then account for it when the aggregate relationship is specified.

What is the reason for the supposed downward orientation of the curve? The answer given by elementary courses in economics looks disputable to me, and not only because of the multiplier phenomenon. It claims that profit maximization leads the firm to pick the level of its demand for labour so that the marginal productivity of labour is equal to the real wage rate; the downward orientation then follows from the assertion that the marginal productivity is a decreasing function of the labour input. A precise discussion of the argument would be too long here (see, however, chapter 6 and Malinvaud, 1991). Its main deficiency comes from the absence of any distinction as to the context within which it is meant to apply, in particular from the lack of a precise reference to the time horizon at issue. The change in labour input described by the downward orientation is intimately linked to investment, i.e. to the renewal and extension of productive capacities; it plays a significant role only if the horizon is not too close. It then occurs both because the substitution of capital for labour is all the more important as the wage rate is higher and because firms are all the more cautious in the choice of their capacity as the expected profit margin is more modest.

If we want to make an accurate discussion about the significance of the main determinants of the demand for labour in unemployment diagnosis and forecasting, we must then distinguish between the short and the long run.

(ii) For short-run macroeconomic analysis there is in practice a good degree of agreement on how we ought to proceed, as I argued in the first chapter. One uses as a reference the Keynesian theory as it was first clarified, then amended and complemented, particularly for open economies. One benefits from empirical knowledge about business fluctuations, a knowledge that is still very unsatisfactory in many respects but was nevertheless made more secure by many econometric studies. Statistical information is widely collected, diffused and scrutinized so that changes in current trends are quickly identified. Even though the outcome in forecasting has not much accuracy and is even on occasions frankly mistaken, there is no general recommendation to make about this work except to say that one should keep investigating the main macroeconomic relationships with about the same methodology. But particular attention should be given here to the formation of the demand for labour within this short-term macroeconomic analysis.

As a first approximation we may accept a very simple relation linking fluctuations of the demand for labour to those of the demand for goods. This relation, estimated on many time series, is sufficiently robust for it to have received names: 'the productivity cycle' in France and 'Okun's Law' in the United States. It implies an important distributed lag in the adaptation of employment to output, partly because the first effect of a shock in the demand for goods concerns average hours of work, partly because an important fraction of employment is a quasi-fixed factor of production and, even for the remaining fraction, some labour hoarding occurs.

One must recognize that this law is only approximate and at times fails to materialize exactly as expected. Some economists are moreover worried by the fact that it does not seem to fit perfectly within the theory as currently taught. They now claim we should better understand the 'transmission mechanism' of product demand shocks to the demand for labour (see in particular section 5 in Lindbeck, 1992). One can only agree with the intention of any research project aiming at improving knowledge of such an important phenomenon. But I believe the theoretical difficulty is to a large extent artificial. It disappears in particular if one makes the hypothesis that the supply of goods by firms is rationed in the short run on their output market. While this hypothesis is admittedly extreme, appropriate theoretical specifications should come close to it, for instance when they account for the market power of the firm.

Relying only on Okun's Law is tantamount to assuming that the curve of the macroeconomic graph I previously discussed is upward sloping; indeed the income effect of changes in the wage rate occurs within the determination of the aggregate demand for goods from which the law is applied. One may well wonder, however, whether there are no other significant short-run effects coming from changes in the real wage rate and acting on the demand for labour. At the aggregate level such effects could conceivably come through substitution of labour for natural or imported resources, or even for the use of little productive existing equipment; they could also come through a variation in the supply of goods by firms serving sellers' markets. All these effects would tend to make our curve less upward sloping. But the global result is likely to remain small enough not to reverse the direction. Indeed, most econometric studies found no significant short-run effect of the wage rate, once the aggregate demand for goods was introduced into the regression.

(iii) Medium-term diagnosis is less secure. It is so not only because of the natural difficulty of forecasting farther ahead, but also because there is less agreement among experts about the kind of analysis to be applied. I hold fairly precise ideas coming from my theoretical reflections as well as from observation of medium-term trends in our countries. But I must recognize that these ideas, which I shall now expose, are not all widely expressed. They contain nothing that would be revolutionary; but many of my colleagues do not pay much attention to some of these ideas because they do not see why there should exist a particular kind of analysis in order to deal with the medium run, i.e. with horizons of some five to fifteen years. For some economists long-run competitive analysis would suffice because equilibrium would be quickly reached, at least with freely operating market forces; experts should either limit their message to the conditions required for free competition, or add projections based on growth models with flexible prices and wages. For other economists the medium run would be correctly treated with the same Keynesian analytical apparatus that proved to be appropriate for the short run.

According to my views, medium-run diagnosis of the demand for labour should be based on a theory explaining the variations of this demand as a function of changes in the real wage rate and of changes in a few other variables having at least the same degree of autonomy. By being based on a theory I do not mean it contains ready-made answers, but rather it may be used as a reference both for the choice of the indicators, whose trends ought to be carefully observed and projected, and for the method leading to a synthetic diagnosis.

Theoretical ideas first permit the classification of the relevant autonomous factors according to the main locus in the economic system where they connect with the demand for labour. Leaving aside for the moment changes in the real wage rate, I see four loci of connection:

— some well known autonomous factors act on the evolution of the demand for goods (changes in foreign demand, decisions concerning taxes, public expenditures or monetary aggregates, etc.); the direction of their action on the demand for labour is clear;

— other autonomous factors act through the growth rate of total factor productivity; anything that increases this rate tends to lower the demand for labour.

The two other groups of autonomous factors act through investment:

— some concern the speed of substitution of capital for labour, mainly because they affect the relative cost of labour with respect to capital; a change in the rates of taxes or social security contributions can lighten the cost of labour and stimulate after a while the demand for labour on new equipment; a rise in long-term interest rates on the world capital market can, after transmission to the home market, increase the cost of capital and similarly stimulate the demand for labour on this account;

— a last group of autonomous factors acts through the growth of productive capacities: where these capacities are expanding fast, businessmen are ready quickly to seize opportunities on domestic or foreign markets; their demand for labour then increases. Increases in capacities depend not only on the expected growth rate of the demand for goods and on the anticipated profitability of production, but also on the degree of confidence with which expectations about future market conditions are accepted; anything that increases business uncertainty also damages, after a while, the demand for labour.

If we now come back to the impact of variations in the real wage rate, we must distinguish three effects: an effect because of the demand for goods, an effect because of the substitution of capital for labour, through the relative cost of labour, and an effect because of capacity building, through the profitability of production. An increase in the real wage has a positive effect on demand, but the two other effects are negative. In order to assess the global effect one must, I believe, be more precise in two respects.

In the first place, both negative effects occur mainly when equipment is replaced or extended; they are therefore slow to appear. In the short run they are weak and the demand effect dominates, as we saw. But the longer the horizon, the more likely it is that the demand effect is superseded by the two negative effects.

In the second place, one must pay attention to business conditions in the current situation of the economy that is supposed to be subject to some autonomous increase in the real wage rate. Indeed, I believe that the effect on productive capacities through profitability much depends on business conditions: when profitability is quite satisfactory, a small increase in wages matters little, expectations about market demand then being almost the exclusive consideration when firms have to decide on their future growth. But when profitability is already poor, when firms worry about their solvency, an increase in the real wage rate inhibits them and leads them to give up projects that would have otherwise been financed. So if, experiencing a situation with a low profitability, one contemplates a real wage increase, one can only expect it to damage the demand for labour in the medium run. In such a case the downward-sloping curve of the graph gives a correct image of the phenomenon.

(iv) As is now clear from the preceding theoretical analysis, I believe a medium-term diagnosis must distinguish between the two dimensions of investment, one concerning the substitution of capital for labour ('capital deepening'), the other the growth of productive capacities ('capital widening'). You notice that I systematically associate to the first dimension a diagnosis on the relative cost of labour with respect to capital and to the second dimension a diagnosis on profitability.[5] This is why I believe that, for

[5] Chapter 7 will show that, rigorously speaking, this simple association is valid only for special cases. But it provides more generally an appropriate first approximation.

medium-term diagnosis on employment, we ought to have available two indicators, one on the relative cost, another on profitability. Even better, considering conceptual and statistical difficulties, we would find it useful to have two groups of alternative indicators.

If I insist here, it is because neither the relative cost of labour with respect to capital nor the profitability of production is easily measured. The collection of the required data is far from complete now. Moreover there are conceptual difficulties, which have already been discussed in the theoretical literature but that statisticians have seldom studied seriously. These difficulties for instance concern the notion of opportunity cost, to be applied for the definition of the cost of capital, and the notion of real profitability, which must be corrected for the bias introduced by inflation in our accounting practice. It is not the place to dwell on these questions of measurement. But I must stress here how important it would be for our diagnoses to have regular estimates of the indicators in question. I may illustrate this point by considering what can now be said about the evolution of the relative cost of labour in Europe during recent decades.

In conformity with the required substitution of capital for labour during the rapid full-employment growth of the 1960s, the relative cost of labour with respect to capital was then increasing. The increase accelerated in the early 1970s up to the middle of the decade, even after the first oil shock. The relative cost remained roughly constant at a high level until the early 1980s, when high real interest rates and wage restraint combined their effects for a reversal of the previous trend. For a few years this reversal seemed to have no impact, labour saving investments remaining predominant; some macroeconomists then said that the former relation between relative costs and the input mix had been disrupted. It turned out that this was erroneous; not only does it now appear on recent data that the capital–labour substitution slowed down; but, as was shown for France by Henry, Leroux and Muet (1988), the observed evolution may be explained by delays in the adjustment of capital to slower growth and by a change in the trend of the industrial composition of output, a change that reacted on the observed overall input mix. Two lessons seem to follow. First, the putty-clay model, which unfortunately is less fashionable in macroeconomics than one might have expected when it was introduced, remains the proper reference for medium-run analysis of the production sector. Second, macroeconomists should always wonder about the possibility of aggregation bias in their aggregate arguments.

(v) In my theoretical discussion of the medium run I listed, among the potential autonomous factors of the demand for labour, some that could act through total factor productivity. I then said that anything that increases the growth rate of this productivity had a negative effect on the evolution of the demand for labour; this statement may have looked paradoxical. If we now pay attention to the relation, we must first be clear on its meaning. An increase in productivity would mean a decrease in the cost per unit of output if it were not exactly matched by an increase in the price of inputs. Since real cost changes were considered independently, I was implicitly referring in my somewhat paradoxical statement to cases when such an exact matching was supposed to occur. Let us keep that in mind.

As is well known, the precise scrutiny of economic growth left unexplained an important residual, corresponding to the trend of productivity of all identified factors of production. Since it is unexplained, this trend cannot be forecast except by mechanical and more or less-sophisticated extrapolations (see chapter 1). The uncertainty of this operation directly reacts on the forecast of the demand for labour. It is sometimes presented as a flaw of macro-economics as if it could have been avoided. The sensible conclusion is rather that we should go on scrutinizing productivity growth trends, their changes and their disparities. I do not expect a quantum jump in our degree of understanding but at least a better factual knowledge.[6] From the present viewpoint, the most significant observation made by the empirical analysis of economic growth was the slowdown of the trend of productivity.

The academic literature about this issue during the last two decades will, I am afraid, give no pride to economists when it is read again with the benefit of hindsight. Issues about the so-called

[6] The 'endogenous' growth theories that were launched by Romer (1986) seem to claim they will provide a quantum jump. But their relevance for expert diagnosis is still to be demonstrated.

productivity puzzles will probably appear to have been too hastily raised, even before an accurate measurement of the slowdown was feasible. Too many loose explanations were hastily given. Fortunately practitioners in charge of employment diagnosis kept cool heads and did not pay too much attention to this literature. (Indeed resisting intellectual fashions is a motto of those engaged in expert diagnosis; there are good reasons for that.)

Among the explanations given was a supposed rigidification of economic operations. But the analysis did not go far into the scrutiny of the macroeconomic phenomenon and devoted most of its attention to the political economy of rigidification. For our discussion of unemployment diagnosis it is significant to note that the productivity slowdown seems to have been the most pronounced in economies that are said to remain the most flexible. France may be taken as an opposite case, because of the barriers to flexibility that results from its labour laws and regulations: the productivity slowdown in France was more progressive and less marked than elsewhere; some may even argue that this is related to the fact that unemployment rose more and more quickly. The implication of this comment should be that the relationship between flexibility and the demand for labour deserves serious attention.

From what we have seen so far it appears first and foremost that the relationship is quite complex and that various forms of flexibility may matter for different reasons. If one does not want to go into details, one may start from the unifying principle that a reduction in flexibility means an increase in adjustment costs. It then has a first general effect, namely to increase overall costs and to reduce profitability, which plays a role discussed earlier. The second general effect is to slow down adaptations: adaptations to the composition of the demand for goods, adaptations to the composition of the supply of labour, adaptations of the level of employment to the quantity of labour required for production. These three kinds of adaptations play different roles in our analysis: slowing down the first type means damaging competitiveness, hence profitability; slowing down the second means increasing mismatch on the labour market, hence frictional unemployment; slowing down the third means lengthening the lag of Okun's Law, thus mainly changing the short-run dynamics of employment.

The macroeconomic framework proposed in this lecture may miss significant aspects of the relation between flexibility and unemployment. It may be argued for instance that institutional barriers to flexibility do not much matter for qualified labour, which is a quasi-fixed factor of production, but may on the contrary matter much for unqualified labour, whose excess supply is particularly acute in recessions. It may be argued also that I did not pay enough attention to the possibility of increasing or contracting employment without significantly changing capital equipment, mainly by increasing or contracting provision of low value-added services both within firms and for their customers; this possibility may be particularly relevant when we consider unqualified labour and impediments to flexibility that load the effective cost of this type of labour.

Notwithstanding all the complications just alluded to, and the resulting uncertainty of an objective diagnosis, the general wisdom in Europe seems to be that rigidities are responsible for part of present unemployment. Governments then face a serious dilemma because there is then contradiction between two aims that labour market institutions ought to achieve: flexibility and worker protection. This dilemma is vividly exemplified by the regulations concerning the type of labour market segmentation previously discussed.

Securing stable employment for workers was a dominant objective of legislators and governments trying to implement an important aspect of European social philosophy. In most European countries temporary contracts are strictly regulated, with the exception of the UK and Ireland. France is not an extreme case, rules there being more lenient than in Germany and Italy (Blanchot, 1990). The objective of these national regulations is to impose conditions for employers to be allowed to use labour on temporary rather than permanent contracts; for instance it would be unlawful to keep the same employee for long by simply renewing his or her temporary contract at each ending.

On the other hand, it was admitted about a decade ago that the European economies were handicapped by excessive rigidities and that they were too slow to adapt to changes in economic conditions, which was considered in part responsible for a loss of competitiveness and a high level of unemployment. To restore flexibility became an important objective; labour regulations that prevented employment from quickly adapting were reconsidered; the case of temporary contracts was particularly scrutinized since freedom of employers and protection of employees were hard to reconcile.

Some of the French statistical evolutions are easily traced to regulation changes that were so motivated. For instance the series on the number of workers employed in interim work shows an increase from 100,000 to 200,000 in the second half of the 1970s as business conditions were deteriorating; after a tightening of the rules the number of interim jobs decreased to 100,000 again at the end of 1984; then the government revised its views and regulations, becoming less hostile to this form of employment: the number involved increased to 300,000 at the end of 1989.

The way in which the conflict is resolved so reacts on the importance of market segmentation. Economists ought to assess the resulting tradeoffs. Unfortunately, in this case as in many others concerning the choice of institutions, we seem to lack operational tools for even a rough assessment. Each of us tends to react according to his or her, hardly rational, confidence in one form of society or another.

(vi) At the end of this lecture a natural conclusion may be briefly to assess the medium-term evolution of the demand for labour in Western Europe during the last twenty years. This summary will be presented without its numerical justifications, which would take too long to give, but it will be reminiscent of the theoretical ideas I explained earlier. Three periods will be considered: 1970–77, 1977–83 and 1983–90. In each case the terminal year will be compared with the initial year.

The first period, which ends in 1977 for convenience, was of course mainly marked by the depressing impact of the first oil shock and by the increased uncertainty of the world environment after the breakdown of the Bretton Woods system. Each country had to reduce the demand for labour, notwithstanding the stimulating economic policies that somewhat alleviated the depression. It is noteworthy that, facing this depression, real wages exhibited a strong inertia. I explain it by saying that, during most of the 1970s, the depressing effect of a low demand for labour was counteracted by a wage push coming from the social malaise that ended the long period of fast growth; during those years employers were ready to grant generous pay rises in order to avoid other troubles.

The second period going from 1977 to 1983 experienced a strong deflation due not only to the second oil shock but also to the reversal of the stance of macroeconomic policies, with the resulting jump in real interest rates. At that time the overall depression of the demand for goods and labour stopped the rise in real wage rates and even the rise in real labour costs, notwithstanding an increase in the burden of social security. This was not sufficient, however, to compensate for the strong drop in profitability that resulted from the rise in interest rates. Investment then fell sharply.

The third period, from 1983 to 1990, benefited from the increase in world demand induced by the American expansionary policy and by the decrease in oil prices, and this notwithstanding the dampening effect of international indebtedness. In some countries this period also experienced a moderation of wage claims that was remarkable concerning the increase in the demand for labour. This moderation ought probably to be explained not only by continuing high rates of unemployment but also by a change in collective attitudes that gave more strength to employers in wage bargains. The demand for labour benefited from the earlier decrease of the relative cost of labour with respect to capital and certainly also from the revival of profitability, although not much as yet because of natural lags.

This brief and compact account is neither surprising nor original. But this is its virtue. Our fellow citizens have the right to request that we economists provide them with diagnoses on which we all agree. We know that this requires persistent work within a general framework recognized as appropriate and with the use of similarly confirmed analytical approaches.

References

O. Ashenfelter and R. Layard (1985) (eds.), *Handbook of Labor Economics*, North Holland, Amsterdam.

C. Bean, R. Layard and S. Nickell (1986), 'Unemployment', *Economica*, Supplement, 53(210(S)).

W. Beveridge (1944), *Full Employment in a Free Society*, George Allen & Unwin, London.

M. Blanchot (1990), 'Le triomphe du travail temporaire', *Eurépargne*, 43.

M. Cézard and J.-L. Heller (1988), 'Les formes traditionnelles d'emploi salarié reculent', *Economie et Statistique*, 215, pp. 15–23.

J.-P. Danthine, C. Bean, P. Bernholz and E. Malinvaud (1990), *European Labour Markets: A Long Run View*, CEPS, Brussels.

W. Dickens and K. Lang (1988), 'The reemergence of segmented labor market theory', *American Economic Review*, 78, Papers and Proceedings, pp. 129–34.

DMS (1987), 'La recherche du carré magique', *Economie et Statistique*, 195.

M. Elbaum (1988), 'Stages, emplois et salaires d'embauche: l'insertion des jeunes à quel prix?', *Economie et Statistique*, 211, pp. 5–21.

M. Glaude and J.-P. Jarousse (1988), 'L'horizon des jeunes salariés dans leur entreprise', *Economie et Statistique*, 211, 23–41.

J.-L. Heller (1986), 'Emplois précaires, stages: des emplois faute de mieux', *Economie et Statistique*, 193–4, pp. 27–35.

J. Henry, V. Leroux and P.-A. Muet (1988), 'Coût relatif capital–travail et substitution: existe-t-il encore un lien?', *Observations et diagnostics économiques*, 24.

R. Jackman, C. Pissarides and S. Savouri (1990), 'Labour market policies and unemployment', *Economic Policy*, 11, pp. 449–90.

A. Lindbeck (1992), 'Macroeconomic theory and the labor market', *European Economic Review*, 36(2).

E. Malinvaud (1984), *Mass Unemployment*, Basil Blackwell, Oxford, translated in Italian as *La Disoccupazione di Massa*, Laterza, Bari, 1986.

(1988), 'Chômage et croissance des capacités de production', *Rassegna di Statistiche de Lavora*, 1, pp. 7–16.

(1991), 'A medium term employment equilibrium', in W. Barnett, B. Cornet, C. d'Aspremont, J. Gabszewicz and A. Mas-Colell (eds.), *Equilibrium Theory and Applications*, Cambridge University Press, Cambridge, pp. 219–37.

P. Romer (1986), 'Increasing returns and long-run growth', *Journal of Political Economy*, 94, pp. 1002–37.

C. Thélot (1985), 'Les traits majeurs du chômage depuis vingt ans', *Economie et Statistique*, 183, pp. 37–59.

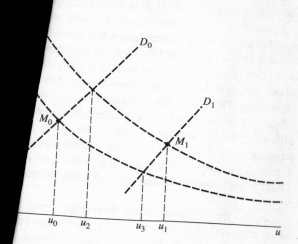

an equally say that $u_3 - u_0$ must be attributed to equilibrium and $u_1 - u_3$ to increased frictional t.

decompositions are possible. The most natural seems e derived from defining what the levels of frictional nt u_f are in periods 0 and 1, and to do this we need to D when total labour supply and demand are equal t is when D is a 45° line through the origin. In figure 5.2, $u_1 - u_0$ in the unemployment rate can be decomposed due to increased frictional unemployment and $(u_1 - u_{f_0})$ due to increased general disequilibrium in the labour

be wrong, however, to think that the last decomposition g conventional about it. The first difficulty stems from the nowhere are statistical data on job vacancies complete. , the measure of v used in practice does not correspond to etical concept discussed here. In order to use statistical this problem, one must then assume that there exists a

5

The Beveridge curve

To what extent can we explain increased unemployment by workers' lack of mobility and reduced economic incentives that used to drive people rapidly either to take a job or to leave the labour force? Finding an objective and convincing answer to this question is essential for a better understanding of the respective roles of the many factors which might have influenced the rise in unemployment in Europe.

The question fits within the framework of a more basic consideration: to distinguish, in the growth of unemployment, what comes from factors affecting frictional unemployment, as opposed to those directly reflecting the general disequilibrium between labour supply and demand.

I have the feeling that our methodology remains too uncertain on how we ought to make such a distinction. Personally speaking, I happen to probe among, if not the choice of fundamental concepts, at least the choice of specifications which should then serve as reference to give a precise meaning to the distinction, and make possible its econometric application.

This chapter, in which I mainly consider the theoretical analysis preliminary to answering the question put at the beginning, expresses my feeling my way, dissatisfied as I am on reading some of the articles trying to identify the role of mobility and economic incentives in the rise of unemployment in various countries.

1. Frictional unemployment and general disequilibrium

Frictional unemployment is normally considered as unemployment that cannot be reduced by purely macroeconomic measures of

Translated by Fatemeh Shadman-Mehta. First given at the 1986 annual meeting of the Association Française des Sciences Economiques (Malinvaud, 1987).

stimulating total demand for labour. Such a definition indeed emphasizes the distinction mentioned earlier, but also attributes to it some unambiguity which is lacking. In fact, any definition of frictional unemployment assumes a convention. The most convenient way of stating the convention refers to what we can call 'the Beveridge curve'. In fact, what is important is to locate, explain or predict the shifting of the Beveridge curve; the measurement of frictional unemployment itself seems secondary.

Let N denote the labour force, also called active population, and let it be identified with labour supply.[1] Let U be the level of unemployment and L that of employment:

$$N = L + U. \tag{1}$$

Similarly, let V denote the number of vacancies. The natural definition of labour demand[2] is:

$$D = L + V. \tag{2}$$

The unemployment rate u is by definition equal to the ratio of U to N. It is common practice to define the job vacancy rate v as the ratio of V to L. With this definition, the following equation results directly from (1) and (2):

$$(1 - u)(1 + v) = \frac{D}{N} \tag{3}$$

and D/N may be taken as a measure of the labour market tightness. Here, it will be more convenient to define the vacancy rate v as the ratio of V to N, leading to the equation:

$$1 - u + v = \frac{D}{N}. \tag{4}$$

Given the sizes of u and v, this change of definition and the substitution of (4) for (3) are clearly of little importance.

In a plane where u appears on the x-axis and v on the y-axis,

[1] Here, I am quite deliberately ignoring questions related to duration of work. It would obviously be better to measure N, U, L, V and D in terms of man-hours. While possible, it would introduce unfamiliar complications; properly explaining them would only render this chapter cumbersome.

[2] Identification of labour supply with the labour force and of labour demand with the sum of employment and vacancies is a simplification. This chapter should be read as complementary with chapter 4 where the simplification was not made, but the discussion did not cover quite the same ground as here and was analytically less precise.

equatio
position
labour s
from inc
(see figur

At any
and its repr
representati
complex syst
discussed in s
in the determi
labour deman
eliminating $D/$
relation betwee
This relation ca
ponding curve C
depicts a link bet
which is independ
market.

Clearly, the posi
exogenous variables
observed a stability i
on many observations
progressively.[3] An up
taken place in many cou
importance of the graph
distinction to be made
general disequilibrium, p
example that at two differe
are M_0 and M_1, with corre
(see figure 5.1). If the Beve
can determine what would
date 0 if the position of the cu
u_2 be this rate. In the variation
to an increase in frictional un
general disequilibrium between
in fact another, equally valid
referring to the Beveridge curv

[3] See for instance Jackman, Pissarides

Figure 5.1

known: one
increased dis
unemploymen

Still other
to be the on
unemployme
look at line
$(D = N)$, tha
the increase
into $u_{f_1} - u$
$u_{f_1}) - (u_0 -$
market.

It would
has nothin
fact that
Therefore
the theor
data for

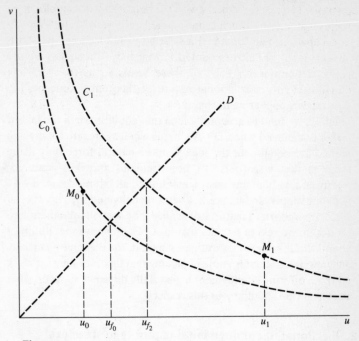

Figure 5.2

constant relationship between the statistical measure and the theoretical concept, a constant proportion for instance (less than 1). In a
figure drawn on the basis of statistical measures of u and v, one
would have to take into account the distortion introduced in job
vacancies; but the distortion isn't known very well. One solution is
to replace line D of figure 5.2 by a line $v = ku$ with a lower slope, the
coefficient k being chosen at best.

Moreover, the theoretical concepts themselves are based on
conventions. These are well known with respect to the active
population, employment and unemployment, all concepts for which
statisticians make a special effort to stick to rigorously defined
conventions. I have accepted here an additional convention of
taking labour supply as being identical to active population,
although one could also say that some 'discouraged workers' should
also be considered as part of the work force. If, given good-quality
data, we tried to make the measure of job vacancies rigorous, then
the conventions inherent in their definition would also become

apparent. To retain symmetry with the definition of unemployment implies that any job which is unoccupied and available for immediate occupation, and for which a salaried or non-salaried person is actively sought, should be counted as a vacancy. But we still require precise definitions for each of these terms so as to avoid any ambiguity. (The conventional nature of theoretical concepts has other aspects appearing in chapter 4.)

Finally, we tend to accept the idea that equilibrium in the labour market is achieved when $D = N$, that is when aggregate supply and demand are equal. But the idea would have full force only if the labour market were perfectly homogeneous and if it achieved, directly and without any cost, a meeting of all labour demand with all labour supply. In fact market heterogeneity and the necessity of search are important features of reality, and we will take them into account in the rest of our discussion. Consequently, the notion of general equilibrium also mitigates and it too becomes partially conventional. Let us also note in passing that those looking for work and those offering employment have totally different views on what the convention should be in this respect.

2. Frictional unemployment due purely to structural diversity

Two alternative theoretical approaches have been used to study frictional unemployment. One approach accepts the multiplicity and diversity of labour markets, each with their own disequilibrium. The other approach analyses the way in which the unemployed search for jobs and firms with vacant posts look for employees. I will consider each of these approaches in turn, as if it alone explained reality.

To begin with, therefore, let us assume there are n distinct homogeneous labour markets, and that on each of them matching of supply and demand takes place directly and immediately. On the other hand, let us also assume that there is no spillover of unsatisfied supply or demand between markets. Such assumptions are obviously quite strong; but they make the analysis clear and simple.

Empirically, distinction between markets would involve two main characteristics: the place and the job specification. A particular market refers to a given job specification in a given town or region. If N_i and D_i denote labour supply and demand respectively in market i, then the global variables obviously satisfy the following relations

$$N = \sum_{i=1}^{n} N_i, \quad D = \sum_{i=1}^{n} D_i. \tag{5}$$

Similar relations apply to employment E_i, unemployment U_i, and vacancies V_i. The assumptions made when defining markets imply:

$$L_i = \text{Min}\{D_i, N_i\}, \tag{6}$$

$$U_i = \text{Min}\{N_i - D_i, 0\}, \tag{7}$$

$$V_i = \text{Min}\{D_i - N_i, 0\}. \tag{8}$$

The following equality results immediately:

$$V_i - U_i = D_i - N_i \tag{9}$$

which gives (4) when aggregated.

Describing the state of the market would be equivalent to giving the values of the $2n$ numbers D_i and N_i. But at the aggregate level one only needs to know the statistical distribution of the pairs (D_i, N_i) in the n markets. This is in fact sufficient for the determination of the aggregate variables D, N, U, V, L, and therefore also the rates u and v.

Intuitively, one can agree that a Beveridge curve is drawn from points (u, v) obtained from statistical distributions which have different means, but the same relative dispersion: the link between u and v, as depicted by the curve, is then independent of the overall market disequilibrium, which is characterized by the mean of the distribution. On the other hand, the link, i.e. the position of the curve, depends on the relative dispersion. The greater this relative dispersion, the higher will the Beveridge curve be placed. For example when $D = N$, the average of the discrepancies $D_i - N_i$ is zero; but the greater the dispersion, the more frequent will be large positive values of U_i or V_i, and this will lead to larger values for U and V.

I will not try to derive here the general analytical form that results from the hypothesis of a fixed relative dispersion for the distributions of the pairs (D_i, N_i). The method is similar to the one followed in Malinvaud (1980).

We can consider, for example, the case where labour supply happens to be the same N/n in all basic markets, and where the statistical distribution of labour demands, despite being discrete, is close to a normal distribution with means $(1-\mu)N/n$ and standard deviation $\sigma N/n$. It can then be shown that the unemployment rate is approximately equal to:

$$u = \sigma\varphi\left(\frac{\mu}{\sigma}\right) + \mu\phi\left(\frac{\mu}{\sigma}\right) \tag{10}$$

where φ and ϕ are the density function and the cumulative distribution function respectively of the standard normal distribution. Equation (4) now becomes:

$$u - v = \mu. \tag{11}$$

Eliminating μ between equations (10) and (11) leads to the equation of the Beveridge curve:

$$u = \sigma\varphi\left(\frac{u-v}{\sigma}\right) + (u-v)\,\phi\left(\frac{u-v}{\sigma}\right). \tag{12}$$

We can see immediately that this curve crosses the 45° line at the point:

$$u = v = \frac{\sigma}{\sqrt{2\pi}}. \tag{13}$$

The higher the value of σ, that is the greater the dispersion of labour demands, the higher will this point be.

A similar case, which is less special and no doubt more adequate, has been studied by Lambert (1988); this is the case where the statistical distribution of the (D_i, N_i)s is approximately log-normal. He finds the following equation:

$$L = [D^{-\rho} + N^{-\rho}]^{-1/\rho} \tag{14}$$

where the parameter ρ is related to the dispersion of the log-normal distribution. Simple operations, using equation (4) in particular, lead to the following equation for the Beveridge curve:

$$(1-u)^{-\rho} = 1 + (1-u+v)^{-\rho}. \tag{15}$$

The curve crosses the 45° line at the point:

$$u = v = 1 - \left(\frac{1}{2}\right)^{1/\rho}. \tag{16}$$

This point is also placed higher up if the value of ρ is larger.

3. Mobility and reduction in frictional unemployment

It is often thought that one way to reduce unemployment is to increase mobility of workers and jobs. The argument put forward most frequently is simple: the difference between the structure of labour demands and labour supplies, each distributed over partitioned markets, leaves some unutilized employment possibilities; if some of the demands or supplies could switch from one market to another, some of these possibilities could materialize. One can see that this remedy for reducing unemployment is more effective in intermediary situations rather than extreme cases. Moreover, one ought not to conclude that all mobility does indeed reduce unemployment.

To study this question, the easiest thing is to consider the case where increased mobility means the fusion of some previously separate elementary markets. If a merged market which has become perfectly homogeneous is regrouping two or more elementary markets which were in opposite forms of disequilibrium, its disequilibrium will be less than the sum of the disequilibria of the markets it is regrouping. Any remaining unemployment will have been reduced by the sum of the number of vacancies which might have existed in some of the elementary markets. For example, if people were willing to work farther away from their homes, or to change their residence more frequently in order to find work, there would be fewer vacancies wherever the number of jobs was growing rapidly; the result would be less aggregate unemployment.

It is intuitively clear, however, that this phenomenon can only have limited scope if there are only few elementary markets where job vacancies persist. In other words it has little effect in situations of mass unemployment. Without trying to prove a general proposition in this respect, we can look back at the example mentioned above of elementary markets of equal size where labour demand is distributed normally. If we now assume that the elementary markets merge together in pairs, in a totally random manner, then labour demand will still be normally distributed in the regrouped markets, but will have a new mean of $2(1-\mu)N/n$ and a new standard deviation of $\sqrt{2}\sigma N/n$. The unemployment rate will no longer be as in equation (10) but will be:

$$u = \frac{\sigma}{\sqrt{2}} \varphi \left(\frac{\mu\sqrt{2}}{\sigma} \right) + \mu\phi \left(\frac{\mu\sqrt{2}}{\sigma} \right). \tag{17}$$

The decrease in the unemployment rate will be greater not only if structural dispersion is higher, but also if μ/σ is closer to zero, that is if total labour demand is closer to total labour supply (in equation (10), the derivative of the expression on the right hand with respect to σ happens to be equal to $\varphi(\frac{\mu}{\sigma})$ and this is maximized at $\mu=0$ precisely).

But mobility should not always be regarded as bringing about the fusion of previously separate markets. An equally frequent case is when unsatisfied demand or supply switches from one market to another. For instance, if a firm cannot find a worker with the required qualifications, it may be satisfied with someone who has close qualifications. A person may accept a job for which she is overqualified for lack of something better. A young person may take a job in Paris rather than in his home region or in the South as he would have preferred.

To understand the effect of mobility caused by switching, we can consider the case in which it systematically occurs on the supply side between two markets. Assume that labour demands are specific to markets 1 and 2, and labour supply in market 2 cannot switch to market 1, but excess supply in market 1 switches to market 2.

It is clear that if there is excess supply in both markets, this mobility will not reduce unemployment; it may on the other hand cause unemployment of suppliers in market 1 to be transferred to those of market 2. This is observed when unqualified workers find themselves excluded from the market because qualified workers accept jobs below their qualification level. The assumed mobility due to switching will only reduce unemployment if there is excess demand in market 2 (this is for instance the case for some types of job in the Paris region).

In this analysis of the effect of increased mobility on unemployment, supply N_i and demand D_i in the elementary markets are assumed to be given and constant. The reasoning is done as if the only possible effect must be on frictional unemployment. In fact, increased mobility may improve productivity. It may allow a better match of jobs to the qualifications of those holding them. It may improve transmission of technical knowledge and diffusion of lessons learned from past experiences elsewhere. The final effect of such productivity improvements on employment depends on induced changes in labour demand and means a move along the Beveridge curve, rather than a shift of the curve.

Even when limiting ourselves to asking whether a behavioural modification with regards to mobility has caused a shift in the Beveridge curve, the answer is not very simple. The reason is that observed changes in mobility may be due to changes in the general economic conditions in which agents find themselves just as easily as they may be due to behavioural modifications. For instance, the observed reduction in mobility in France over the past decade may simply be the result of generalized unemployment. We saw earlier that when the same type of disequilibrium prevails in most markets, the effect of increased dispersion between markets is weak. For the same reason, observed mobility in such a case is slight even if the disposition to move is normal.

To conclude therefore that changes in mobility signalled a shift of the French Beveridge curve, one would need other kinds of proof. These could relate to demographic effects, or even to increased attachment to homes which are increasingly owner-occupied.

Finally, referring back to the effects of structural diversity discussed in section 2, we should also consider whether increases in particular components of the mismatch between the distributions of labour supply and labour demand have played a role. We will do this in section 7.

4. Frictional unemployment resulting from search duration

Putting structural diversity on one side now, we can study the effect of the inevitable search times the unemployed spend looking for employment and the employers spend trying to fill vacant posts. It is convenient to start with a simple model.

Given that the unemployed and vacancies are now assumed to constitute two homogeneous sets, it is rather natural to assume a Poisson distribution for the probability of an unemployed person coming across an acceptable job or leaving the labour force. Let p denote this probability per unit of time; p is constant by definition of the Poisson distribution. The probability of being still unemployed after a duration of t is then $\exp\{-pt\}$ and the average duration of unemployment is $1/p$. If e denotes the rate of entry into unemployment per unit of time, as compared to the employed active population L, then the rate of entry of the active population N is $e(1-u)$. The product of this rate by the average duration of unemployment gives the unemployment rate u in a stationary regime where p, e and u remain constant:

$$u = \frac{e(1-u)}{p}. \tag{18}$$

Solving for u, we obtain:

$$u = \frac{e}{e+p}. \tag{19}$$

It may be suggested that this model is not realistic because observation has systematically shown that the frequency of exiting from unemployment decreases with the spell of time already spent in unemployment, contrary to what a Poisson distribution would imply (Clark and Summers, 1979; Salais, 1980). However, this effect can be simply due to the heterogeneity of the population of workers and the unemployed, each homogeneous subpopulation giving rise to its own probability.[4] Hence, if we ignore heterogeneity for the moment, the criticism is no longer necessarily valid.

To derive a Beveridge curve from equation (19), we must remember the definition of the curve. It is obtained by elimination of the labour market tightness variable D/N from a system of equations that represents the joint determination of u and v. For stationary regimes, this system is made up of equations (4) and (19), to which must be added those concerning the determination of the rates e and p of entry into and exit from unemployment. Analysis of data on labour markets flows now provides good information on how the rates vary with various kinds of changes, in particular with changes in labour market tightness (Burda and Wyplosz, 1990).

The entry rate e depends partly on demographic factors and activity behaviour (entry of youth or return of women to the job market). It also depends on institutional changes such as the more common use of temporary contracts which forces some people to search for jobs more frequently. Finally, it depends on general economic conditions. A downturn in the economy is often characterized by an increase in the number of lay-offs, which is only partially compensated by a decrease in the number of voluntary resignations.[5] Changes in

---

[4] It turns out to be very difficult to identify the effect of heterogeneity on the aggregate unemployment exit rate (Thélot, 1988; Heckman, 1991).

[5] This variation of the entry rate with labour market tightness explains why I cannot accept the definition given to the Beveridge curve by Pissarides (1990).

economic conditions, that is in the disequilibrium between labour supply and demand, are represented here by the ratio D/N, which may be denoted as θ. We may then write e as a decreasing function of θ, and as an increasing function of an exogenous variable z_1 representing exogenous factors acting on the entry rate: $e(\theta, z_1)$.

Observation shows that, on the contrary, the exit rate p is a slowly increasing function of labour market tightness θ. It also depends on exogenous factors captured here by an exogenous variable z_2, so that we can write $p(\theta, z_2)$. The exogenous factors here are mainly the intensity of the search efforts of employers and the unemployed. There are also institutional changes such as the more frequent use by employers of contracts with limited duration.

The Beveridge curve is obtained by elimination of θ from (4) and (19) where the functional forms of e and p are taken into account. Differentiation of these equations and functions leads to a local representation of the Beveridge curve, that is to the linear relation linking small changes du, dv, dz_1 and dz_2 in the variables, once change $d\theta$ in labour market tightness has been eliminated. The linear relation may be written as:

$$a\,du + b\,dv = (1-u)\,e_z'\,dz_1 - up_z'\,dz_2 \tag{20}$$

with

$$a = e + (1-u)\,e_\theta' + p - up_\theta', \tag{21}$$

$$b = up_\theta' - (1-u)\,e_\theta'. \tag{22}$$

The derivatives p_θ' and e_θ' being respectively positive and negative, the coefficient b is clearly positive. This is also true of coefficient a because the elasticities of e and p with respect to θ are too small for the contrary. The Beveridge curve has indeed a negative slope. Equation (20) shows that the curve shifts to the right when z_1 increases or z_2 decreases, as for instance when the participation of women in the labour force increases or when the search intensity decreases.

This definition of the Beveridge curve has the problem of being derived from the analysis of stationary regimes. The speed of convergence towards such a regime is of course rather high, given

His equation (1.4) is identical to our equation (19); but when deriving the Beveridge curve from it, Pissarides assumes the exit rate to remain constant along the curve.

that the unemployed population gets renewed rather quickly. Nevertheless, we can be almost certain that the Beveridge curve determined from the comparison of stationary regimes is not exactly appropriate for the transitory phases of the convergence towards such a regime. We can expect that a sudden deterioration in the general economic conditions will rapidly entail a reduction in job vacancies and an increase in entries into unemployment, whereas the effect on the unemployment rate will be more progressive. Therefore, to begin with, the move takes place below the Beveridge curve. An improvement in general economic conditions on the other hand will first give rise to moves above the Beveridge curve. Such a sequence of events is also compatible both with the implications of the assumed Poisson process and with the observations made on the basis of available statistical data.

5. Search unemployment and mismatch unemployment

A separate analysis of two main explanatory factors of frictional unemployment, structural mismatch and search duration, ought to pave the way for their simultaneous consideration. I have the feeling that it is not so simple.

The first idea to come to mind is to imagine frictional unemployment as the sum of two terms. The rate of frictional unemployment u_f could be written as the sum of the rate of search unemployment u_r and the rate of structural mismatch unemployment u_s. We would then know that such a decomposition, as for the definition of frictional unemployment, would be just a convention. But this would in no way nullify its relevance to the analysis.

The relevance might stem from the fact that a good model specification to determine u_f would result directly from modelling u_r on the one hand and u_s on the other. In other words, one could directly take up the propositions presented in sections 2 and 4. For instance u_r could be determined by an equation like (19) and u_s by (10).

A closer look, however, reveals that it is not so simple to combine the factors 'search duration' and 'structural mismatch'. Modelling as suggested here would lead to a different solution: apply the search duration model to each of the micromarkets i discussed in section 2; replace equations (6), (7) and (8) by other equations taking into account the fact that, even in a given micromarket, the confrontation between labour supply and labour demand is not direct; aggregate as a final step.

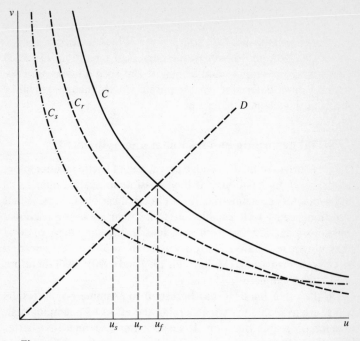

Figure 5.3

I will not attempt to apply this solution here, not even on a particular specification. I will only propose an intuitive conjecture: the rate of frictional unemployment must be less than the rate we would obtain by a simple addition of a rate of search unemployment, determined with the assumption of perfect homogeneity in the labour market, and a rate of mismatch unemployment, determined under the assumption that search duration in each micromarket is zero. In other words, search unemployment and mismatch unemployment do not add up.

Figure 5.3 illustrates this phenomenon with three different Beveridge curves: the effective curve C and two hypothetical curves, C_r if there was no heterogeneity in labour supplies and demands, and C_s if in each micromarket labour supplies and demands were met instantly. Curve C is indeed placed above the other two, but not as much as would be implied by additivity $u_f = u_r + u_s$.

The implication of this remark should not, however, be exaggerated. For an analysis of small variations in frictional unemployment (or a 'local' study as mathematicians would put it), one can accept an approximation where the effects of various causes acting on frictional unemployment are added, some of these causes relating to search duration and others to the degree of structural mismatch between labour supplies and demands. But such a linear approximation cannot determine what is purely search unemployment or purely mismatch unemployment.

6. Social protection and frictional unemployment

Once the origin of the Beveridge curve, and of frictional unemployment, is well understood, it is then possible to analyse their shifts and to quantify econometrically the effects of various factors. A first assertion seems well established today: variations in frictional unemployment are far from sufficient to explain those of total unemployment. I have already discussed the proofs of this assertion on two other occasions (Malinvaud, 1984 and 1990); I will therefore not repeat them here.

On the other hand, it may be useful to examine briefly results which are available today concerning the effect of unemployment benefits on search duration. It seems natural enough that better benefits are likely to make the unemployed more demanding before accepting a job and also slow down exit from the active population, thus increasing frictional unemployment. The only question is how important is this phenomenon. Today, the answer to this question can be given more precisely than ten years ago.

To start with, it is worth distinguishing this question clearly from a similar question: the influence of unemployment insurance on total unemployment. This insurance must have some effect on the macroeconomic determinants of disequilibrium unemployment; both through its effects on variations of aggregate demand for goods and on profitability of production (Malinvaud, 1985).

It is not possible to identify clearly the effect on frictional unemployment with econometric analysis of time series: this effect is too weak and the measure of frictional unemployment too uncertain. On the other hand, various studies on cross-sections of individual data have provided relatively clear, though imprecise conclusions.[6]

[6] Clark and Summers (1982), Lynch (1983), Atkinson et al. (1984), Feldstein and Poterba (1984), Moffitt (1985), Narendranathan et al. (1985).

Unemployment benefits do have some positive effect on frequencies of entry into unemployment (from inactivity) and some negative effect on frequencies of exit from unemployment. However, these effects are only significant as far as the youth are concerned. In fact, the various studies, which have used different data sets and addressed slightly different questions, and hence considered different specifications, have not yet put forward a coherent and complete representation of the phenomena at work.

No doubt, our social security systems will in future be revised over and over again, in the attempt to achieve the best balance between the contradictory objectives of equity and efficiency. It is therefore essential to pursue the progress achieved recently in this domain rather than contenting ourselves with the results obtained for the United Kingdom or the United States.

7. What about shifts of the Beveridge curve in France?

What can we say today about shifts of the Beveridge curve in France, that is to say about the role of frictional unemployment in the increase of unemployment? Unfortunately, a lot less than would be desirable for providing a complete explanation of this insistent phenomenon.[7]

The first difficulty arises from the poor nature of the statistical indicators of the number of job vacancies. These indicators are undoubtedly useful for analysing the short run. But for medium-term comparisons which are more of interest to us, they must be regarded with scepticism. The indicator used most widely is the number of job offers registered at the Agence Nationale Pour l'Emploi (ANPE). It is common knowledge that this statistic greatly underestimates the number of job vacancies. We know that the underestimation was reduced during the period 1967 to 1973, when many new offices of this agency were being set up. But unfortunately, it may also have varied because of changes in ANPE's efforts in collecting the offers or changes in employers' expectations as regards the aid they could receive from the agency for recruitments.

---

[7] I have already considered this question on pp. 212–13 of Malinvaud (1986). I am returning to it briefly, not only to give it a natural complement, but also to clarify my conclusions. In particular, I would like to incorporate, in a more satisfactory manner, the Manpower-Expansion index and especially the points proposed by Thélot (1985).

Another indicator, called the Manpower-Expansion index, results from a reading of job offers in twenty-three daily newspapers and in various weeklies (all professions and all qualifications aggregated). But this indicator may also be subject to some drift due to changes in employers' habits of advertising their offers.[8] In any case, the variations in this index are very different from those of job offers registered at ANPE. From 1969 to 1973 the index went down by 13 per cent whereas the official agency statistic was multiplied by 3.2. From 1973 to 1979 the variations are − 33 per cent and − 65 per cent respectively; then from 1979 to 1985, − 16 per cent and − 48 per cent (all figures relate to annual averages).

Direct comparison of these statistics with unemployment rates gives ambiguous conclusions. Even after correcting for biases due to the setting up of the Agency, the official series suggests a clear upward shift of the Beveridge curve from 1969 to 1973, whereas the unemployment rate went up by about 20 per cent. Since 1973 on the other hand, this indicator suggests that the Beveridge curve has remained stable. (Thélot (1985) notes, however, that a comparison of female unemployment rates with vacancies in the service sector suggests an upward drift in the curve.) On the contrary, the Manpower-Expansion index gives the impression that the curve has clearly shifted between 1973 and 1979 as opposed to the four previous years, and even more clearly from 1979 to 1985.

In brief, it is hard to conclude on the basis of this purely descriptive approach, even though it seems to lend support to the idea that frictional unemployment has somewhat increased. But there is certainly no hope that one might be able to measure the asserted increase in this way. It is therefore necessary to study more closely the possible causes for increased frictional unemployment.

As far as the factors affecting structural mismatch are concerned, it would seem that during the period we are interested in, they did not experience a significant change. I have given the proofs of this assertion in Malinvaud (1986). I will not repeat them here; I will just recall the only noticeable exception to this overall stability in the degrees of structural mismatch: since 1975, the discrepancy between labour demand and supply has increased particularly sharply for unskilled labour. This resulted from technological progress and at the

---

[8] I must acknowledge here some clarifications with regards to this index made by Mr Closon, marketing manager at Manpower.

same time from a great effort, which began towards the end of the sixties and continued through the years of crisis, to substitute capital for labour. This fact alone could explain a slow slide of the Beveridge curve.

A modification in the structure of labour supply could also explain such a slide, although it may not have aggravated structural mismatch since it was accompanied by a similar modification in the structure of demand. Labour supply has especially increased for women who have longer search durations than men (lower frequency of exit from unemployment) and also more frequent unemployment spells (higher frequency of entry into unemployment). The share of women in the active population in fact increased from 35 per cent in 1968 to 41 per cent in 1982.

Another feature appears to be increased acceleration in the rotation in the labour market towards the end of the sixties, which would have led to increased frictional unemployment. Thélot attributes this acceleration of market movements on the one hand to intensification of industrial restructuring, and on the other hand to a change of attitude among workers who, even though they were already employed, increasingly looked for other jobs and gave in their notice, even if this entailed a period of unemployment.

It is also highly likely that the more frequent use of limited duration contracts and interim work during the 1980s has led to higher frictional unemployment. This has definitely affected the frequencies of entry into unemployment, and its effect on the frequencies of exit must have been less: the flow of job offers must have increased as a result of this practice, and employers must have moderated their requirements before recruiting; but since workers often prefer permanent posts, they must have searched longer before accepting insecure jobs.

Finally, we must take into account that unemployment benefits have vastly improved from the late sixties to early eighties. As a result, search durations especially for young people must have slightly increased, as we mentioned before. However, this phenomenon has recently reversed its course. Since 1983, unemployment benefits are somewhat reduced, returning to levels just above those of 1975.

Of the five factors that could explain a shift in the Beveridge curve since 1968, one seems to have affected the whole period, two mostly the period before 1975, and two mostly after. On the whole, it is likely that there has been a significant and probably regular shift of the curve. But it is clear that this by itself is totally insufficient to explain the increase in unemployment in France. I hope that others will better succeed in determining the importance of its role.

References

A.B. Atkinson, J. Gomulka, J. Micklewright and N. Rau (1984), 'Unemployment benefit, duration and incentives in Britain: how robust is the evidence?', *Journal of Public Economics*, February–March.

M. Burda and C. Wyplosz (1990), 'Gross labor market flows in Europe: some stylized facts', CEPR discussion paper, 439.

K.B. Clark and L.H. Summers (1979), 'Labor market dynamics and unemployment: a reconsideration', *Brookings Papers on Economic Activity*, 1.

(1982), 'Unemployment insurance and labor market transitions', in M.N. Baily (ed.), *Workers, Jobs and Inflation*, Brookings Institution, Washington.

M. Feldstein and J. Poterba (1984), 'Unemployment insurance and reservation wage', *Journal of Public Economics*, February–March.

J. Heckman (1991), 'Identifying the hand of the past: distinguishing state dependence from heterogeneity', *American Economic Review*, 81(2), pp. 75–9.

R. Jackman, C. Pissarides and S. Savouri (1990), 'Labour market policies and unemployment in the OECD', *Economic Policy*, 11, 449–90.

J.P. Lambert (1988), *Disequilibrium Macroeconomic Models: Theory and Estimation of Rationing Models using Business Survey Data*, Cambridge University Press, Cambridge.

L.M. Lynch (1983), 'Job search and youth unemployment', *Oxford Economic Papers*, November, Supplement.

E. Malinvaud (1980), 'Macroeconomic rationing of employment', in E. Malinvaud and J.-P. Fitoussi, *Unemployment in Western Countries*, Macmillan, London, pp. 173–205.

(1984), *Mass Unemployment*, Basil Blackwell, Oxford.

(1985), 'Unemployment insurance', *The Geneva Papers on Risk and Insurance*, 10, pp. 6–22.

(1986), 'The rise of unemployment in France', *Economica*, Supplement, 53, pp. 198–217.

(1987), 'La courbe de Beveridge', in AFSE, *Flexibilité, mobilité et stimulants économiques*, Nathan, Paris, pp. 59–77.

(1990), 'The labour market in disequilibrium', in A. Barrère (ed.), *Keynesian Economic Policies*, Macmillan, London, pp. 31–52.

R. Moffitt (1985), 'Unemployment insurance and the distribution of unemployment spells', *Journal of Econometrics*, April.

W. Narendranathan, S. Nickell and J. Stern (1985), 'Unemployment benefits revisited', *Economic Journal*, June.

C. Pissarides (1990), *Equilibrium Unemployment Theory*, Basil Blackwell, Oxford.

R. Salais (1980), 'Le chômage: un phénomène de file d'attente', *Economie et Statistique*, 123.

C. Thélot (1985), 'La croissance du chômage depuis 20 ans: une interprétation macroéconomique', *Economie et Statistique*, 183.

(1988), 'La sortie du chômage', in *Essais en l'honneur de E. Malinvaud*, Economica, Paris, pp. 861–93.

6

Real wages and employment – a decade of analysis

I feel greatly honoured to speak here in memory of Josiah Stamp who wanted to promote the development of socio-economic statistics and the progress of economics, two objectives that were also mine. The Lecture should have as its subject 'the application of economics or statistics to a practical problem of general interest'; the members of the Stamp board moreover suggested that I select a theme related to employment. Hoping to comply with their wishes, I intend to discuss what we now know about the role of real wages in the determination of employment.

This is, as we shall see in a moment, an old problem and one about which various schools of economists often disagreed. Ten years ago it again came to the forefront when European wages were said to be too high; the poor employment performances in Europe were said to be caused in part by a wage gap. The question was studied and extensively discussed. Was it solved? Opinions probably vary, but an independent observer would, I am afraid, conclude that in economics fashions are shortlived and interest quickly shifts from one subject to another; the wage gap hypothesis went out of fashion before it was either proved or disproved. It falls to me to remark that the same economist can simultaneously discard the hypothesis and make in his analysis of employment assumptions that, if true, would imply the validity of the hypothesis.

This is a most unfortunate situation. The subject will generally remain as important as it was in the past when Keynes and Rueff disputed about it. The European evolution of the 1970s and 1980s was quite abnormal, hence rich in information context, like a pathological case. Our data base to examine it has an accuracy and a

Stamp Memorial Lecture, delivered before the University of London on Wednesday 23 November 1988.

wealth of details that Josiah Stamp could only dream of. Hence, this subject must remain as an important item on the research agenda of economists.

Even though not conclusive, the past decade of analysis bore fruits about which it is interesting to reflect. Better understanding of the difficulties raised by the question ranks among these fruits. My talk will indeed be devoted to the clarification of issues as much as to the discussion of results. The first half of it will concern concepts and theory; the second will deal with factual knowledge of the phenomena and of their determination.

1. Conceptual issues

I was reassured about the appropriateness of my topic when I discovered that it was closely connected to the one of another Stamp Memorial Lecture, that was given thirty-four years ago by Sir Dennis Robertson (1954) under the simple title 'Wages'. I shall make great use of this previous lecture and quote it extensively, pointing to the distinctions that we now think appropriate to stress, before I explain why Sir Dennis' analysis must receive an important amendment.

I cannot pretend to show the same wit as is found in the presentation of the issues by my famous predecessor. So, I must recommend you to take the pleasure of reading his full text. Moreover, I shall take advantage of the progress of mathematical education to write very few equations and of modern technology to exhibit some graphs, which will, I hope, make the argument easier to follow.

Sir Dennis' analysis

Sir Dennis Robertson discusses what he calls 'the proper wage'. He defines it first 'as being such that any divergence from it of the actual wage will set in motion forces tending to corrective action' (p. 8); but his following text makes it clear that an excess of the actual wage over the proper one will generate unemployment, this being the main 'force tending to corrective action', according to his words.

Any employer, he first explains, will employ just the amount of labour that makes the marginal productivity of labour equal to the wage; since a 'proper balance' is assumed, this condition will define the proper wage. For clarity we may give to this argument a familiar mathematical expression. If the available amounts of labour and capital are denoted respectively by L and K, the production y that can be obtained from them may be written as:

$$y = f(L, K). \tag{1}$$

The proper wage w is, at this stage, determined by the marginal productivity of labour, i.e. by the derivative of the production function f with respect to labour:

$$w = \frac{\delta f(L, K)}{\delta L}, \tag{2}$$

more precisely, by the value taken by this derivative when L and K are equal to the available amounts of these two factors of production.

Sir Dennis then writes: 'If the level established by collective bargaining exceeds this level, a number of people will . . . lose their jobs' (p. 9). In order to be accurate I must recognize that he adds here a condition of 'general monetary stability' that looks to me obscure at this stage and about which I shall have more to say later. But he goes on, commenting on the meaning that should be given to the rule that I expressed with equation (2).

He acknowledges that, in the operation of modern manufacturing processes, it often happens that adding or withdrawing some amount of labour would make no sense: one more man would be useless, and on the contrary 'the whole process would come to a stop' if one tried to withdraw one man; in other words, the marginal productivity of labour is not well defined. To this argument he answers that one must 'allow *time* for (his) principle to work itself out. The techniques of production are not immutable; and if labour is dear you will see them altering in such a way as to employ less of it, while if it is cheap you will see them altering so as to employ more of it' (p. 9). He then asks us 'to distinguish between the immediately or ostensibly proper wage, and that which is truly proper in the long run. It is the latter which the wage fixed by collective bargaining will tend to come up to but must not exceed.' 'If labour is too greedy the *quantity* of capital equipment will be increased in such a way as to throw some labour out of work – over a certain range capital will be *substituted* for labour' (p. 10).

You notice that the argument is then not precisely the same as before. We started with the idea that, taking the wage into account, employers would use the corresponding amount of labour, determined in our words by the solution L of equation (2) for a given amount K of capital. The fundamental phenomenon could be visualized by the simple figure 6.1 showing the type of causation. But Sir Dennis explains that looking at this phenomenon would give us 'the immediately or ostensibly proper wage', not the one 'which is truly proper in the long run'. For the latter we must consider a longer-term phenomenon in which capital is determined as a function of the wage, i.e. we must consider figure 6.2 rather than figure 6.1.

$$w \to L \qquad\qquad\qquad w \to K \to L$$

Figure 6.1   **Figure 6.2**

But this is not yet the whole story. We may indeed wonder whether 'the level of profits turned out by the principle is in any sense the right one' (p. 11). Sir Dennis writes that there are 'strong forces at work tending to make it correspond not only with the *value* of the services rendered, but with their *cost*. In other words . . . if you encroach on [this level of profits] beyond a point you will find that there is a drying up of the willingness to save, to display enterprise, to take the risks of tapping new markets, introducing new processes, devising new products, on which the ability to pay wages ultimately depends' (p. 11).

Clearly, this is again not quite the same argument as before. Whereas it still concerns capital accumulation and still implies a causation of the type represented in figure 6.2 this is no longer the same dimension of capital that is involved; this is no longer its intensity and the substitution of capital for labour, but rather its width and its productive capacity. One suspects here that these two dimensions do not play exactly the same role in our analysis and ought to be better distinguished. I shall indeed distinguish them in a moment.

At this point I should like to draw your attention to another Stamp Memorial Lecture that was given still earlier, in 1949, and by one of the great economists of the interwar period, Professor A.C. Pigou (1949). The lecture had the title 'Wage statistics and wage policy'. It also discussed what would happen if wages were too high.

Pigou wrote: 'One penalty is increased unemployment' (p. 29). It is probably small in the short run. 'But from a long-run standpoint the provision of business capacity and of capital is liable to be checked – perhaps in a cumulative way – so that presently aggregate output and the aggregate earnings of labour are both injured. Marshall regarded this kind of reaction as very serious.' Let me stop this digression here. I shall not quote Marshall, who could not give any Stamp Memorial Lecture, and I must return to Robertson. He adds two considerations to his analysis.

First he comes back on the condition of general monetary stability. He writes that, if the economy experiences deflation, 'even if we think that from a long-run point of view the money wage is too high, we should not wish to see it fall, for fear of reinforcing the downward drift of monetary demand, and intensifying trade depression without producing any appreciable fall in *real* wage rates' (p. 13).

There are two ideas in this quotation. First, what really matters is the proper real wage and acting on the nominal wage rate may not be effective for correcting the real wage. Since my concern is not policy but analysis, I shall not pay any more attention to this point, although I recognize it may be quite significant in practice. Second, the real wage reacts on the demand for goods. This reaction should be fully integrated into the analysis; I shall come back to it in a moment.

Sir Dennis finally recognizes that his presentation of the subject has been restricted to the theoretical case of a closed economy and that in reality the country is dependent upon earning its imports by foreign trade. He then adds: 'In such a country it is less difficult than it would be in a closed one to attach a fairly clear meaning to the concept of a proper wage, and more dangerous to be landed with an improperly high one' (p. 14). The argument then is that export performances provide a test as to whether the real wage is the proper one.

I am ready, probably more than many others, to accept the idea of such a test, but with one important proviso that strongly limits the usefulness of the test. Export performances depend on productive capacities, hence on past wages, but relatively little on the present wage. In other words, competitiveness should be recognized as an important element of a full analysis; but considering an open economy does not reduce the relevance of a scrutiny as to whether present real wages are appropriate to the needs of capital accumulation in this economy.

Complements

It appears at this point that Sir Dennis has given us many important elements of the conceptual system required for an assessment of the European situation of the 1970s and 1980s, but that we must still complement his analysis in three directions. First, while his initial principle and my equation (2) were quite clear, it now appears that they are not exactly what is meant; but the exact implications of the considerations presented after the statement of this initial principle have not been drawn in such a way as to give us a fully articulated system; we must figure out what this system ought to be. Second, Sir Dennis has not fully dealt with the interplay between wages, demand and employment; I am therefore going to tackle this issue right away. Third, as all of you certainly realized as I was speaking, other elements, which have not been mentioned so far, also have to come into play.

Opponents to the wage austerity in Europe during the last two decades forcefully argued that the dependence of investment on real wages did not involve only cost calculations but also the impact of wages on the demand for goods. Under the commonly accepted hypothesis that I shall consider more precisely later on, wage restraint depresses the demand for goods and is then unfavourable for investment. Many economists have taken this effect as being stronger than the ones discussed so far. Considering the presence of this effect as serious, other economists arguing in favour of wage austerity added the recommendation that fiscal and monetary policies be stimulating so as to maintain a satisfactory level of aggregate demand.[1] Perhaps one should also read Sir Dennis' condition of 'general monetary stability' in a similar fashion.

Recognizing the important role of the demand for goods, which I am now denoting as d, we must add it on to figure 6.2 so as to obtain figure 6.3. Actually the depressing impact of lower wages on demand is likely to operate more quickly than the favourable impact of lower labour costs on investment. This is the reason why I am drawing a shorter arrow from w to d than directly from w to K.

[1] See Meade (1982); Malinvaud (1982).

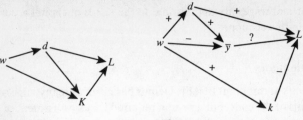

Figure 6.3   Figure 6.4

But figure 6.3 is not yet quite appropriate as a summary presentation of the various arguments we have heard up to this point. Clarity requires that we distinguish the two dimensions of capital, its productive capacity that I am denoting as $\bar{y}$ and its capital intensity k, which is directly related to the factor proportion. We then arrive at figure 6.4. We may mark on it the sign of the various effects following from an increase of the real wage rate: this increase stimulates the demand for goods, hence the demand for labour; it may slow down the growth of productive capacity, hence also the growth of the demand for labour; it accelerates the substitution of capital for labour, and this again reduces employment.

The interest of figure 6.4 in comparison to figure 6.3 is to show the ambiguous nature of the effect of wages on investment. Too high wages should stimulate too much investment intended to increase labour productivity but they may also induce too little investment intended to increase productive capacity. In the end, however, both effects result in a too low demand for labour. The argument applies when these effects are not dominated by the two favourable impacts induced by the expansion of the demand for goods.

We now see what is required in order to test the wage gap hypothesis. We should examine whether, in the conditions prevailing in Europe, a lower real wage rate would have induced a larger gain of employment through capital accumulation than the loss generated by the depression of demand. In order to decide this issue, we should measure each one of the seven effects appearing on figure 6.4. I insist on the idea that what is needed is not a general proposition that would apply in all times and places but a specific conclusion for the case of Western Europe in the 1970s and early 1980s. In all likelihood some of the seven effects are quite non-linear so that the final outcome of a decrease in real wages is likely to depend to a great extent on the situation to which it applies.

The problem is even a bit more complex because one must define the time horizon: the effect after one year may be quite different from the one after five or ten. Indeed, it is a reasonable hypothesis, substantiated by a good deal of econometric work, that the effect of wages on the demand for goods is rapid, whereas the building of new productive capacities requires more time, and a sizable effect of cost changes on actual factor proportions still more time. As the disposition of figure 6.4 is meant to illustrate, the short-term final outcome of a wage increase is likely to be favourable to employment, whereas the opposite might hold for what Sir Dennis called the long run, but I prefer to call the medium run. Clearly, our concern here is the latter time horizon, the one that corresponds to the observed duration of European unemployment.

On what might the elasticities of the medium-term effects depend? They might depend on the values of all the relevant variables. First come the variables appearing in figure 6.4: the result will differ depending on whether one starts from a situation of full employment or of mass unemployment, whether one starts from already high or low real wages, and so on. But one should also consider other variables that have not been mentioned so far, because they are implicitly assumed to be independent of the real wage rate. Such an assumption is never quite true. It must be viewed as one of the elements defining the analytical framework within which one has chosen to work. Particularly noteworthy here is the level of the so-called autonomous demand for goods, which might consist of demand on foreign markets, government demand, even those parts of consumer and business demand that are not directly related to real wage rates. Also noteworthy is the real capital cost, that I am denoting as r: for a given real wage a higher capital cost means both a different relative factor cost and a lower profit margin, both of which might conceivably react on the force of some of our effects.

In the end it falls to observation to tell us how strong is each one of the seven effects we identified and on what its strength depends. Theoretical reflection may, however, help us to progress a bit more, since it can be based on hypotheses that observation has otherwise found justified as first approximations.

In particular I may present a simple form of two equations resulting from an analysis of the decisions of business firms concerning their capital equipment. Taking the irreversibility of these decisions and the uncertainty of future demand into account, one may derive equations showing how productive capacity and capital intensity will change when the mean expected demand d and the real costs w and r change by δd, δw and δr. Under conditions that I shall spell out in chapter 7, one finds the following approximate equations for the changes $\delta \bar{y}$ and δk of the two dimensions of capital:

$$\frac{\delta \bar{y}}{\bar{y}} = \alpha \, \frac{\delta q}{q} + \frac{\delta d}{d}, \tag{3}$$

$$\frac{\delta k}{k} = \beta \, \frac{\delta c}{c}, \tag{4}$$

in which c is the relative factor cost w/r whereas $\delta q/q$ is a measure of the impact of the changes in real factor costs on the profitability of production.

One sees that productive capacity ought to have a unit of elasticity with respect to expected demand and an elasticity α with respect to profitability; capital intensity ought to have an elasticity β with respect to relative factor cost, this latter elasticity being proportional to the familiar elasticity of substitution between the two factors. The elasticity α, on the other hand, is likely to be small when one starts from a situation of good profitability, real labour and capital costs being then low; in that case the effect shown on figure 6.4 by the arrow going from w to $\bar{y}$ is weak, which should imply that productive capacity increases with the wage rate when the demand effect is taken into account. The elasticity α is on the contrary likely to be high when one starts from a situation of low profitability, then productive capacity should decrease as a function of the real wage. One may suspect that this second case applied when and where in Europe profitability had particularly deteriorated, for instance in France in the early 1980s.

I shall end my theoretical discussion here. It is clear that I did not exhaust the questions raised by the relationship between wages and employment. In particular I did not speak about the structure of wages as between qualifications, industries or regions. The lack of flexibility in this structure may have played a role on European unemployment. Similarly the existence of a high minimum wage in some countries may be taken as responsible for a part of youth unemployment. But discussing these questions would lead us too far out of our main subject.

2. Evaluation of the main effects

Turning my attention now to the empirical and econometric side of our enquiry, I should like to assess what we know about the force of the various links that we identified and about the final medium-term effect of real wages on employment. My conclusion will be that our present knowledge leaves much to be desired, but I should like to give some hints as to how it might be improved.

Needless to say, I do not pretend to survey all the econometric work that is relevant for our question. I should rather like first to take a brief look at economic history, second to point to the difficulties of measuring such notions as wage gap or profitability, third to consider what we can expect to learn from direct regressions between employment and the real wage, then briefly to examine where we now stand in our estimation of the roles of the determinants for each of the four variables appearing in figure 6.4: demand for goods d, productive capacity $\bar{y}$, capital intensity k, finally the demand for labour; when doing so, I shall of course limit attention to the determinants that are relevant for our problem.

Some history

For the British the question of knowing whether real wages are responsible for unemployment is not new. In his lecture Sir Dennis Robertson was concerned by the fact that 'between 1938 and 1953 the ratio of the national wage-bill to the net national income at factor cost increased by 16 per cent' (p. 11). He also quoted some results of Professor Phelps Brown showing a similar 14 per cent jump between 1913 and 1924 in the ratio of wages to total income. Presenting them Professor Phelps Brown had raised, but not answered, the question of knowing whether the reduction 'in the return to risk-capital and enterprise' had not set up 'reactions on the side of supply'.

Indeed, economic historians should look particularly at what I believe to have been the relatively poor British economic performances during the 1920s and again during the 1950s and 1960s. To what extent should these results be attributed to too high wages and to a resulting too low business profitability? When looking some years ago at comparative figures for manufacturing between England and France during the 1960s, I was impressed to see that profit rates were significantly lower in the United Kingdom and real interest rates higher (King and Mairesse, 1984).

Another interesting question for economic historians, in ten years from now, will be to wonder about the role of high real interest rates in the second part of the 1980s, while business profit rates have recovered what would otherwise appear as satisfactory levels. Answering this question may be as instructive as answering the one that motivates my lecture: are too high real wages in the 1970s and early 1980s responsible in part for the present European unemployment?

Proper measurement

When these historical questions are being raised one cannot but wonder whether our statistics give us the best indicators for assessing the situation. Such a query cannot be pushed aside in a Stamp Lecture. What I have in mind here is not the accuracy of the basic figures; they are not perfect, but could hardly be improved in general without extensive and costly new surveys. In any case we are now much better equipped with statistics than when Stamp and Robertson were working. I am rather thinking about the proper definitions to be given to summary indicators on which we concentrate our attention and which we may enter into our econometric fits.

The difficulties concerning these definitions reflect the hesitations of our conceptual analysis. First we must decide how we correct for inflation. I shall not insist on the issue today since it was discussed in the UK more than anywhere else for business accounting[2] and since the best reference for the application to national accounting is due to the present chief of the UK Central Statistical Office, my former colleague, Jack Hibbert (1983). I shall simply regret that clarification of the conceptual issues did not lead to a more frequent use in practice of data that would have been corrected for inflation. The discussion showed that such data have, still more than others, to rely on conventions that cannot avoid some degree of arbitrariness. But,

[2] Walton (1978).

when inflation significantly varies, lack of correction leads to more misleading figures than would result from a conventional correction.

The second question is to know whether we can and ought to give a regular measure of the wage gap, which was so much spoken of some years ago. Serious work was devoted to this measurement, in particular in the book by Bruno and Sachs (1985) and in an article by J. Artus (1984). This work was recently surveyed in a very useful and thoughtful article by Helliwell (1988), from which I draw the following personal conclusions.

Any well-founded measure of the wage gap must rely on an explicit representation of the supply decisions taken by enterprises, in particular on a specification of their production function. Given the present stage of our macroeconomic knowledge, there are various possibilities for this representation and this specification; since they lead to significantly different results, no formula for measuring the wage gap is likely to get wide recognition. In other words, pretending to give a regular evaluation of the wage gap would be premature now, and still, I am afraid, for some years to come.

I hasten to add that the research work surveyed by Helliwell was, however, quite instructive. Not only did it clarify the issues that must be faced when trying to define a measure, and show in particular why the share of wages in national income is very far from giving an appropriate indicator, it also gave support to the idea that in some countries for a number of years wages were indeed excessive.

Without trying to get into technicalities, I must insist on what I consider to be a basic flaw of these attempts. The wage gap has a natural definition; it is the difference between the current real wage rate and a value that would be consistent with a satisfactory level of the demand for labour by firms, assuming the demand for goods would otherwise be satisfactory. The hypothetical value of the real wage rate that is considered would permit an equilibrium of the labour market, while the current value is claimed to prevent it. Clearly, the contemplated equilibrium is not meant to be implemented in the short run, but after several years at least, so that productive capacities are themselves consistent with it. Now, all the measures so far proposed assumed the capital stock to remain fixed at its current state; they then considered a hypothetical increase of the demand for labour working on this capital stock. This assumption removes from the representation of the demand for labour what I consider to be its main proximate medium-term determinant besides the demand for goods, namely adaptation of the capital stock (see figure 6.4).

Since the wage share does not provide an appropriate indicator and the wage gap is still a too debatable concept, the best solution is, I believe, to consider the profit rate in production and to compare its evolution to that of the real interest rate. By so doing one directly faces the question raised by Professor Phelps Brown, namely whether too high real wages have not led to a too sharp reduction in the return to risk-capital and enterprise, thus setting up reactions on the supply side.

The definitions of the rate of profit and the real interest rate, as well as the meaning of the comparison between them, need to be carefully studied. Trying to do so here would take me too far away from my theme.[3] I shall simply remark that the ratio between the profit rate in production and the real interest rate provides a simple profitability indicator; it is somewhat similar to the ratio q introduced by Professor Tobin (1969), except that it refers to past rather than expected profits, the implicit assumption being that the two are strongly correlated. Equation (3) has shown the significance of this indicator, since the equation states that productive capacities should react to the impact that changes in real remuneration rates have on the indicator.

The demand for labour as a reduced equation

I must now turn my attention to the econometric work of the past decade about the effects concerning us here. Most of this work entertained the idea that the relevant elasticity of the demand for labour with respect to the real wage could be confidently estimated by a direct fit of a simple equation. I must try to explain clearly here why I view with suspicion the results so obtained.

In the background often lies the simple vision of a supply and demand graph with the real wage plotted as abscissa, the amounts of labour supplied and demanded appear as given by two familiar

[3] I have already discussed one method for the evaluation of the two relevant rates in my *Essais sur la théorie du chômage*, 1983. I shall take up the question again on another occasion.

curves crossing each other. This graph had been dismissed in the 1930s as misleading, but is unfortunately reappearing in macro-economic teaching nowadays. It was thought to be misleading mostly because it conveyed the idea of an equilibrium of the labour market, an idea which would rule out the possibility that real wages were too high. But I see also a danger in thinking that one can identify a somewhat stable simple relation in which the real wage would be the main argument of the demand for labour.

The discussion in the first part of this talk should have shown that the role of real wages takes several routes and is to a large extent indirect and delayed. An accurate representation requires as many equations as there are links in the phenomenon. Of course a full system of equations representing this structure could be solved to give a demand for labour as a function of all its determinants. This demand for labour would then be what econometricians call a reduced equation. But in the first place, the exact meaning of the wage elasticity appearing in this equation would depend on the full specification of the structural system, in particular on its scope, i.e. on the causal links that it takes into account and on those that it assumes to be negligible, in particular also on its full list of exogenous variables. In the second place direct estimation of this reduced equation is likely not only to run the risk of an important bias but also to turn out to be quite inefficient.

In order to make these comments a little more specific, I may refer to the results presented in two recent articles. The first one by Bean, Layard and Nickell (1986) actually considers a two-equation system that is supposed to determine employment and the real wage simultaneously; a graph, pretty much in the spirit of the one I mentioned a moment ago, can be drawn in the real wage–employment plane to show how this system works. From my present point of view what matters is to note that the first equation is supposed to represent the determination of the demand for labour from the real wage rate and a number of exogenous variables. Fitted for eighteen countries on the annual data of the period 1953–83 the system leads to what are claimed to be 'fairly sensible' results with a marked depressing effect of real wage on employment, the long-run elasticity being 'somewhere between one half and unity in absolute value'. From France in particular this elasticity would be about -0.6, the 5 per cent confidence interval being estimated to be $(-0.3; -0.9)$.

The article by P. Artus (1987) concerns only France and fits on quarterly data for the period 1963–83; but a large number of tests and estimations are presented on alternative models that have been used in the econometric literature during the past decade, including one model that is claimed to be borrowed from Layard, Nickell and Jackman. In all estimations the equation of the demand for labour shows an insignificant or very weak effect of the real wage. French readers are certainly puzzled since this article was published just after a presentation by Bean (1987) of the results he obtained with Layard and Nickell.

These conflicting results are typical of the state of the literature that so addressed directly the estimation of the elasticity of the demand for labour with respect to the real wage, although I must recognize that the two groups of results just reported appear to be at the opposite ends of the interval covered by estimates found for this elasticity with the approach I am now discussing.

Part of the difficulty with this approach comes from the need to specify short-term effects and their timing simultaneously with longer-term ones. The econometrician is then led to think much more about the current decisions of firms than about their longer-term strategy. Indeed, most specifications of the demand for labour used in this kind of work take capital as an exogenous variable, as it is indeed done in the article by Bean, Layard and Nickell. The long-term elasticity that is derived from the fit then has a very ambiguous meaning.[4]

Even if the specification would be about right for representing both the long and short-term effects, I suspect that the fits would be biased in favour of the identification and correct estimation of factors that act with a short lag and against the recognition of those that act more slowly. I have presented elsewhere the reasons for my suspicion about this difficulty that more generally concerns the usefulness of time series econometrics for the estimation of long-run effects (Malinvaud, 1989).

---

[4] Actually, beyond the elaborate dynamic structure and the exogeneity of capital I still have one more difficulty with the model selected by Bean, Layard and Nickell, namely the cross-equation restrictions that relate the parameters of the demand for labour to those appearing in the equation determining the real wage. I do not really understand the rationale of these restrictions, which imply in particular that in the long run the unemployment rate depends on the exogenous factors of the demand for goods, but not on the volume of capital, nor on technical progress (time), nor on the size of the labour force.

The difficulty I am now stressing is avoided when the regression of the demand for labour is used simply as a measure of short-term elasticities. It may then be viewed as a true structural equation. I shall now consider it in this spirit, going back to figure 6.4, which will help us to see what econometric estimates are required for answering the main question motivating this talk.

A research agenda

According to figure 6.4 the proximate determinants of the demand for labour would be the demand for goods, the existing productive capacity and the capital intensity. A natural simple form for the relationship would be:

$$L = g(k) \cdot \text{Min}(d, \bar{y}), \tag{5}$$

output being the minimum of demand and capacity, while $g(k)$ would be the labour input coefficient implied by capital intensity k. But I must immediately recognize that this particular relationship and even figure 6.4 are simplifications. A proper specification of the short-term demand for labour will require more than estimation of the function $g(k)$. Let me briefly list some of the reasons why we must be more sophisticated.

First, equation (5) comes from consideration of a representative firm whereas all firms are not similarly constrained, some are constrained by demand, others by capacity, the proportion between the two varying with the macroeconomic situation. Second, technical progress changes the function g through time. Third, adjustment costs and in-firm flexibility of productive operations explain why employment reacts somewhat sluggishly. Fourth, this same flexibility implies that productive capacity is not fully rigid, even in the short run; this means that output and employment will somewhat depend on the current profitability of production, hence on the real unit labour cost.

Something, however, should remain of equation (5). The short-term demand for labour equation should consider capital and the demand for goods as exogenous; it should distinguish the two dimensions of capital: its capacity and its intensity; the demand for goods and capacity should enter non-linearly, in a way that might depend on direct information obtained from firms as to the constraints they are facing. In this last respect, one may hope that the econometric approach recently experimented with by Lambert (1988) will be more commonly applied. One may even entertain the hope that one day we will know how the short-term elasticity of the demand for labour with respect to the real wage rate depends on the degree of capacity utilization.

In any case, figure 6.4 reminds us that knowing the short-term law of the demand for labour is not enough for our objects. We should also know how the real wage rate reacts on the demand for goods and on both the volume and composition of the capital equipment.

I stressed earlier in this talk that shifts in the income distribution can have effects on aggregate demand and that this consideration played an important role in the discussions dealing with the consequences of wage austerity. It is a pity that the econometric characterization of these effects remains so imprecise. I cannot claim to know all the econometric literature that might be relevant for this question. I wrote a piece about it myself (Malinvaud, 1986), concluding that a shift from profits to wages indeed reduces national saving, as stated on figure 6.4. But I did not receive on that occasion much information, except to note that my conclusion was not shared by everybody: in his 1984 book Marglin devotes one long and careful chapter to estimations from quarterly US data for the period 1952–79 with the purpose of answering the present question; but his conclusions are far from clearcut.

Here again, putting emphasis on medium-term phenomena leads to a different assessment than when only short-term effects are considered. In the short run, in particular as long as a significant correlation exists between the type of income earned and the probability of being liquidity constrained, a shift from profits to wages is very likely to increase aggregate demand, because it is likely to lead to an increase in household consumption, and to a larger increase than the limited decrease in investment that will result from the contraction of the financial resources of enterprises. But medium-run effects are much more complex to analyse. They depend in particular on how investment reacts; figure 6.4 itself reminds us that the incentive to substitute capital for labour and the short-term increase in demand may more than compensate the decrease in profits and profitability; whether this occurs or not depends on the respective importance of the various effects; as I reported previously, the theoretical analysis leads us to suspect that compensation will indeed occur when the initial level of profitability was satisfactory and the increase in wages is not too great.

This discussion shows how important it would be for our subject to evaluate precisely the size and timing of the effects concerning productive investment decisions. The econometric literature is abundant but again not as conclusive as we should like it to be.

I first note that it hardly ever distinguishes the two dimensions of capital. You understand by now that I consider this as unfortunate, even though I recognize the difficulties of a precise definition of productive capacity. Let me remind you of my two reasons. On the one hand, since relative costs should act mainly on capital intensity whereas expectations of demand and profitability should act mainly on productive capacity, estimation will more efficiently measure the main effects if it is applied separately to the two dimensions of capital than if they are combined. On the other hand, we ought to know how each one of these dimensions is determined, since they play different roles in the short-term demand for labour. But for the time being, we must draw conclusions from the econometric literature as it is. Here are my conclusions.[5]

The acceleration phenomenon is commonly identified. An increase in demand reacts fairly quickly on expected demand and on the volume of productive capital, perhaps not as fully as the proportionality of equation (3) would imply, but by a similar order of magnitude when medium-term effects are considered.

Although much less precisely estimated, the conjectured impact of relative costs has been identified and often appeared as significant. It was then found weak or spread over a large number of years. This result agrees with the putty-clay notion, which direct knowledge of production techniques also suggests as providing a useful approximation. Considering moreover the available results coming from the econometrics of production function, I believe it is quite safe to conclude that equation (4) approximately applies with a coefficient β which is small for the short-term effect and somewhere between 0.3 and 0.7 for the long-term one (the elasticity of substitution between capital and labour being somewhere between 0.5 and 1).

[5] I am not aware of a good recent survey that I could give as a reference. My conclusions follow from my incomplete reading of the literature of the past thirty years. Among the most recent publications that attracted my attention I may mention in particular here Artus and Muet (1986).

Finally, econometrics gives only weak evidence about the effect of profitability and does not permit me to propose a measure for it today. This is unfortunate but understandable: first, profitability is a forward-looking concept whose measurement raises many problems, even when one is ready, as I am, to accept adaptive expectations as a useful hypothesis for econometric fitting; second, one cannot easily distinguish between the effect of profitability and the short-term impact that past profits have as providing finance for a quick realization of investment projects; third, I explained that the effect of profitability should be strongly non-linear, which of course makes econometric estimation more difficult.

The weak econometric evidence about the existence of the effect mostly, but not exclusively, derives from the work inspired by the q-theory of investment. This work is very recent, so that one may hope that more precise results will progressively emerge from it. The availability of time series covering the full period from the 1960s to the end of the 1980s should soon give us in Europe data bases that should have an interesting information content for our object, since they will trace the consequences of the exceptional dip of business profitability that occurred in our region and of its recent recovery. Hopes are therefore permitted on this score also.

'Travaillez, prenez de la peine'. Such is the first line of the poem in which Jean de La Fontaine tells about a farmer who, when dying, had told his sons that they would find a treasure in his land if they would work hard enough on it; there was no treasure, but hard work produced good harvests and good returns.

The last decade of analysis about the effect of real wages on employment did not lead to the discovery of any treasure and leaves many questions unanswered. However, our knowledge improved, perhaps more than we can realize it today.

In his 1979 presidential address to the American Economic Association, Robert Solow (1980) extensively referred to Pigou's *Theory of Unemployment* (1933), showing in particular how careful Pigou was in explaining the arguments from which he derived his conclusions. Solow quotes one such conclusion concerning the subject of my talk, namely that the elasticity of the demand for labour with respect to the real wage 'cannot, on the least favourable assumption here suggested, be numerically less than -3 and may well be larger than -4' except perhaps in the very shortest run.

Clearly, if Professor Pigou were still with us today, he would retract and change his estimate as well as his argument.

References

J. Artus (1984), 'The disequilibrium real wage hypothesis', *IMF Staff Papers*, June.

P. Artus (1987), 'Salaire réel et emploi', *Revue Economique*, 38(3).

P. Artus and P.-A. Muet (1986), *Investissement et emploi*, Economica, Paris.

C. Bean (1987), 'Salaires, demande et chômage: une perspective internationale', *Revue Economique*, 38(3).

C. Bean, R. Layard and S. Nickell (1986), 'The rise of unemployment: a multi-country study', *Economica*, Supplement, 53(210(5)), 1–22.

M. Bruno and J. Sachs (1985), *Economics of Worldwide Stagflation*, Harvard University Press, Cambridge, MA.

J. Helliwell (1988), 'Comparative macroeconomics of stagflation', *Journal of Economic Literature*, 26, pp. 1–28.

J. Hibbert (1983), *Measuring the Effects of Inflation on Income, Saving and Wealth*, OECD, Paris.

M. King and J. Mairesse (1984), 'Profitability in Britain and France 1956–1975: a comparative study', in D. Holland (ed.), *Measuring Profitability and Capital Costs*, Lexington Books, Heath and Co., Lexington, MA, pp. 221–72.

J.-P. Lambert (1988), *Disequilibrium Macroeconomic Models: Theory and Estimation of Rationing Models using Business Survey Data*, Cambridge University Press, Cambridge.

E. Malinvaud (1982), 'Wages and Unemployment', *Economic Journal*, 92, pp. 1–12.

  (1983), *Essais sur la théorie du chômage*, Calmann-Lévy, Paris.

  (1986), 'Pure profits as forced saving', *Scandinavian Journal of Economics*, 88(1), pp. 109–30.

  (1989), 'Observation in macroeconomic theory building', *European Economic Review*, 33, pp. 205–23.

S. Marglin (1984), *Growth, Distribution and Prices*, Harvard University Press, Cambridge, MA.

J.Meade (1982), 'Domestic stabilisation and the balance of payments', *Lloyds Bank Review*, January.

A.C. Pigou (1933), *The Theory of Unemployment*, Macmillan, London.

  (1949), *Wage Statistics and Wage Policy*, University of London, London.

D. Robertson (1954), *Wages*, University of London, The Athlone Press, London.

R. Solow (1980), 'On theories of unemployment', *American Economic Review*, 70(1), pp. 1–11.

J. Tobin (1969), 'A general equilibrium approach to monetary theory', *Journal of Money, Credit and Banking*, February.

J. Walton (1978), 'Current cost accounting: implications for the definition of measurement of corporate income', *Review of Income and Wealth*, December.

7

Profitability and factor demands under uncertainty

In Paris during the winter of 1943–44 a mathematics student was attracted by economics. Without the guidance of any professor, he was trying to understand various books dealing with this field. One day he entered the little shop of a publisher, rue de la Sorbonne, and bought a book with the fascinating title *Les fondements mathématiques de la stabilisation du mouvement des affaires* (*Mathematical foundations of the stabilization of business fluctuations*).[1] The author was an 'expert temporairement attaché à la Section Financière et au Service des Etudes Economiques de la Société des Nations', J. Tinbergen. As he was studying the book very carefully, this young man could not imagine that forty-five years later he would be given the honour of delivering the Tinbergen Lecture.

Today, then, I am paying tribute to one of my best teachers, one whom I did not bother with questions but who with this book played an important role in my economic education. Probably my approach to economic phenomena was to a significant extent shaped by what I then learned from Jan Tinbergen.

The subject of this lecture concerns what has been the main question motivating my research during the last decade, namely the medium-term relationship between wages and employment. This question concerned Tinbergen fifty years ago and was indeed very much discussed at the time. For instance, he writes in his 1938 book that 'wage policy is not very important for business trends because of the double role played by wages as factors of demand on the one hand, and of production costs on the other. However, wages become important when one considers their impact on the output

Second Tinbergen Lecture, delivered on October 8, 1988, in The Hague for the Royal Netherlands Economic Association, first published in *De Economist*, 137(1) (1989), pp. 2–15.
[1] Tinbergen (1938).

equilibrium level in a country competing on the world market' (pp. 91–2). Similarly, an article published jointly in *Econometrica* in 1939 with Pieter de Wolff provides, as one of its important results, an estimate of the long-run elasticity of the wage rate on the demand for labour (Tinbergen and de Wolff, 1939).

I am not going to discuss today the full system that determines the medium-term impact of the real wage rate on employment, a system that has in particular to take into account the role of wages with respect to the demand for goods. I shall concentrate my attention on what I believe to be the crucial part of this system, namely the part representing the decisions of firms about their capital equipment, with its two dimensions: productive capacity and capital intensity, i.e. the factor proportion implied by its full utilization.

I shall first define the nature and the results of my inquiry. I shall then present the model that I find appropriate for this purpose. The rest of my presentation will be devoted to an outline of a fuller treatment of the model that has been published elsewhere in French (Malinvaud, 1987).

1. An overview

Attention has been given recently in applied as well as in theoretical economics to the relationship between profitability and investment. Discussions on economic policy, in Western Europe in particular, often concerned the question of whether profitability had to be restored in order for investment to increase again, for new competitive productive capacities to be built up and for the demand for labour to expand. On the other hand, often stimulated by the recent progress of disequilibrium economics, macroeconomic theory also considered this subject, which it had surprisingly neglected for so long. However, much remains to be done in order to integrate profitability fully within investment theory.

This integration is now provided by what is called the q theory of investment. According to this theory the amount of productive capital that firms aim at is related to the ratio q between the present value of future profits, expected to result from production, and the cost of this capital. In order to justify the theory, the initial portfolio argument of Tobin (1969) may look somewhat far-fetched and has not been precisely incorporated within the models of producers' decisions. The more recent papers by Yoshikawa (1980) and

Hayashi (1982) refer to adjustment costs that have now become the *deus ex machina* in any theoretical model involving investment. But adjustment costs are certainly not very significant when one considers medium-term phenomena. The core of the explanation must be different.

Non-formalized economic literature has for a long time considered that profits were the rewards of risk-taking by entrepreneurs and that some degree of profitability was required in order for this risk-taking to reach the appropriate level. The theory of factor demands under uncertainty should then exhibit this role of profitability. This is the theory I tried to elaborate, taking uncertainty of future demand and irreversibility of investment as the main reasons explaining why profitability matters.

It should be noted at this stage that, being concerned with medium-term phenomena, I shall neglect here whatever limit the availability of owned or borrowed funds may impose on investment. Past profits are then not important as a source of finance but only to the extent that they explain expected profitability.

In order to introduce my results, I shall use a teaching tool that Tinbergen particularly likes, the arrow scheme representing the directions of causation. My discussion will concern the exact meaning and validity of the vision presented in figure 7.1, according to which productive capacity would depend on profitability and the expected level of the demand for goods, whereas capital intensity would depend on relative factor costs.

Three main conclusions can be drawn from the analysis of a static partial equilibrium model of a representative firm, a model that I shall define precisely in a moment.

In the first place one must be careful when speaking of the role of profitability. The value taken by Tobin's q is endogenous, since it depends not only on exogenous prices and costs but also on capital intensity and on the expected rate of capacity utilization, which varies with productive capacity. Hence, comparative statics properties must take as exogenous not the change in q, but the direct impact that changes in prices and factor costs have on q or, better, an appropriately defined indicator of this impact.

In the second place, the elasticity of productive capacity with respect to profitability varies a great deal, depending on the reference equilibrium. This elasticity increases with uncertainty and

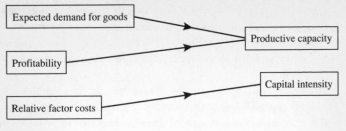

Figure 7.1

would vanish if demand became certain. It also quickly decreases when profitability in the reference equilibrium improves. Hence, the role of profitability exhibits a strong non-linearity.

In the third place, the two central properties are only approximate. Productive capacity does not depend only on profitability and on the random distribution of demand; it also depends somewhat on relative factor costs. Capital intensity does not depend only on relative factor costs; it also depends somewhat on profitability and on the distribution of demand.

2. The production function[2]

When defining any model of the firm, the first problem is to decide how much to allow for the substitutability between labour and capital. Tinbergen was conscious of the problem in 1942 when in *Weltwirtschaftliches Archiv* he treated in parallel two specifications, one with a Cobb–Douglas production function, the other with strict proportionality between labour and capital. Since then we have had the invention of the concept of a putty-clay technology. This is essentially the concept I am using.

The irreversibility of productive capital has two dimensions. When capital is built, not only must specific techniques of production be chosen, but also the size of the productive capacity must be selected. The combination of mobile factors and the maximum feasible output with this capital are then strongly determined.

In order to represent these two features, I shall characterize capital by two variables: its intensity k and its capacity $\bar{y}$. The latter is simply the maximum output that can be obtained from this

---

[2] The specification will be fundamentally the same as in Johansen (1972).

capital, whereas capital intensity is here, by definition, the ratio between the volume K of capital and its capacity:

$$k = \frac{K}{\bar{y}}. \tag{1}$$

Labour will be considered as fully mobile and as being the only other factor of production. As soon as the quantity y of output has been decided, the required labour L will be shown and proportional to it, the production depending, of course, on capital intensity. I shall represent this relationship by:

$$L = yg(k), \qquad 0 \leqq y \leqq \bar{y}. \tag{2}$$

Hence, the four main variables may be divided into two groups: $\bar{y}$ and k to be chosen in advance, y and L to be decided later for the current productive operations. Similarly, one can speak of two production functions.

The *long term production function* applies at full capacity. It is derived from (1) and (2) when $\bar{y} = y$; it then relates L, K and y in the way traditional production functions do, although perhaps in a somewhat unfamiliar manner. It then assumes constant returns to scale, a hypothesis that will be maintained for simplicity throughout the analysis.

The function g, which characterizes ex ante substitutability between capital and labour, is of course decreasing. It will be assumed here to be differentiable. One can easily check the following properties:

— the ex ante marginal rate of substitution between capital and labour is equal to minus the derivative of g, i.e. to $-g'$;
— the ex ante elasticity of substitution between capital and labour is equal to η given by:

$$\eta = \frac{-g'[g - kg']}{kgg''}. \tag{3}$$

The *short term production function* takes $\bar{y}$ and k as given, but no longer assumes equality between output and capacity. It is given by (2) and implies constant returns to scale below capacity. On a graph with L and y being measured on the horizontal and vertical axes, respectively, this production function would be represented by two straight line segments, the one from the origin to $(\bar{L} = \bar{y}g(k), \bar{y})$; the other being horizontal from this point to the right.

The technology assumed here can be said to be 'putty-clay' since it implies ex ante substitutability and ex post complementarity. The static nature of the specifications, however, simplifies matters up to a point that proponents of the putty-clay technology might perhaps refute.

3. The demand function

Attention will be focused on the ex ante choice of capacity and capital intensity. This choice of course depends on the market conditions confronting the representative firm. They will be assumed to correspond to what is now commonly specified in models of monopolistic competition.

The firm is a price taker for its inputs: the unit costs w of labour and r of capital are then exogenous. No rationing exists on factor markets, which means in particular that a labour shortage is not expected. But the firm faces a random demand function for its output. This is specified by a function $S(y, u)$ giving the money value that the sale of output y has when the state of demand is u. As a function of y, S is assumed to be concave. As a function of u, S and its derivative with respect to y are assumed to be non-decreasing.

The ex ante probability distribution of u is assumed to be known by the firm. For simplicity it is specified as depending only on two parameters Eu and h:

$$P(a) = \text{Prob}\{u \leqq a\} = F\left[\frac{a - Eu}{h\,Eu}\right]. \tag{4}$$

Eu may be thought to be the expected value of u and h its coefficient of variation, the function F being kept fixed in the whole analysis. The uncertainty about future demand that is exhibited by this probability distribution may of course in part reflect fluctuations of demand during the period of utilization of capital.

Decisions of the firm are assumed to maximize the expected value of profit:

$$W = S(y, u) - wL - rK. \tag{5}$$

(Malinvaud, 1987, also discusses the case of risk aversion and of insolvency risk.) It is noteworthy that, with this criterion, one can also take the factor costs and the nominal value of the sales function to be random, as long as they are assumed to be stochastically independent of the level of demand u: the notations w and r then refer to the expected values of unit factor costs; similarly $S(y, u)$ refers to the expected value of output y conditional on the state of demand being u.

4. Optimal behaviour

Ex post, knowing $\bar{y}$, k and u, the firm chooses y so as to maximize

$$S(y, u) - wg(k)y \tag{6}$$

subject to $y \leq \bar{y}$. Since S is concave as a function of y, the solution is

$$y = \text{Min}\{\hat{y}, \bar{y}\} \tag{7}$$

where

$$R(\hat{y}, u) \geq wg(k) \geq R^+(\hat{y}, u), \tag{8}$$

$R(y, u)$ and $R^+(y, u)$ being the left and right partial derivatives of $S(y, u)$ with respect to y, i.e. the marginal revenue function. It is assumed that this system (8) has one and only one solution $\hat{y}$ (which amounts in practice to assuming that the labour cost w is not too high).

Ex ante maximization of the expected value of profit W takes as given the short-term behaviour specified by (7) and (8); it then determines capacity $\bar{y}$ and capital intensity k. In order to express the maximization conditions, it is convenient to introduce a new variable $\bar{u}$ characterizing the state of demand for which $\hat{y}$ is just equal to capacity $\bar{y}$. In other words $\bar{u}$ is the solution of:

$$R(\bar{y}, \bar{u}) \geq wg(k) \geq R^+(\bar{y}, \bar{u}). \tag{9}$$

It is assumed to be uniquely determined and is then a function of $\bar{y}$ and k. Equations (7) and (8) then imply that $y = \hat{y}$ when $u < \bar{u}$ and $y = \bar{y}$ when $u \geq \bar{u}$.

The first-order conditions for maximization can then be written as:

$$\int_{\bar{u}}^{\infty} [R(\bar{y}, u) - wg(k)] \, dP(u) = rk \tag{10}$$

$$-T(\bar{y}, k)g'(k) = \frac{r}{w} \tag{11}$$

in which $T(\bar{y}, k)$ is the expected degree of capacity utilization $Ey/\bar{y}$ and can be computed as:

$$T(\bar{y},k) = 1 - P(\bar{u}) + G(\bar{y},k) \tag{12}$$

with

$$G(\bar{y},k) = \frac{1}{\bar{y}} \int_0^{\bar{u}} \hat{y}\,\mathrm{d}P(u). \tag{13}$$

Second-order conditions for maximization are not absolutely innocuous, as shown in Malinvaud (1987), but will here be assumed to hold.

Equations (10) and (11) have clear economic interpretations. Since $R - wg$ is the marginal gross profit, which according to (8) is essentially zero for $u < \bar{u}$, equation (10) means that the capital cost of a unit of capacity must exactly be covered by the expected value of the marginal gross profit. Equation (11) means that the ex ante marginal rate of substitution between capital and labour, corrected for the expected rate of capacity utilization, must be equal to the relative cost of capital with respect to labour.

Equations (10) and (11) determine $\bar{y}$ and k as functions of the parameters, in particular w, r, Eu and h. This determination will be assumed to be unique. The ex ante expected demand for labour EL is then easily derived as:

$$EL = \bar{y}T(\bar{y},k)g(k). \tag{14}$$

It is again a function of the parameters.

The aim of the model is a precise discussion of comparative statics effects: how do $\bar{y}$, k and EL change as functions of w, r, Eu and h? However, a discussion on the general specification turns out to be too cumbersome to be really illuminating. This is why comparative statics properties will be studied here for two particular specifications, which are analytically simple and may be considered as covering the most relevant cases.

5. Comparative statics: the kinked demand curve

Let us first concentrate on the case in which:

$$S(y,u) = p\,\mathrm{Min}\{y,u\} \tag{15}$$

implying

$$R(y,u) = p \text{ if } y \le u. \\ 0 \text{ if } y > u \tag{16}$$

The firm can sell as much as u at the exogenous price p, but it can sell no more. The demand 'curve' has the form of an extreme kink.

The comparative statics properties that follow do not need the kink to be that extreme; they require only that the solution of (8) be $\hat{y} = u$, which here amounts to assuming $p > wg(k)$ but would hold as soon as the marginal revenue would drop at the kink from above $wg(k)$ to below it.

Reasons for the kinked demand curve to provide an interesting approximation in macroeconomics have been given for instance by T. Negishi (1979) and J. Drèze (1979) and will not be repeated here. Price rigidity may provide an additional reason in the context of this paper if randomness of demand is viewed as taking the form of random fluctuations of the demands to be served in future periods.

With the specification (15), equations (10) and (11) take simpler forms:

$$[p - wg(k)][1 - P(\bar{y})] = rk \tag{17}$$

$$-T(\bar{y})g'(k) = \frac{r}{w}, \tag{18}$$

$\bar{u}$ being replaced by $\bar{y}$ and $\hat{y}$ by u in the definitions of the functions T and G.

Differentiation of these two equations gives the system that provides the basis for the comparative statics properties.[3] Easy interpretation of the properties is found when the exogenous infinitesimal changes δp, δw and δr in price and unit costs are replaced by their impacts on the relative cost of capital with respect to labour $c = r/w$ and on the profitability indicator:

$$q = \frac{E(py - wL)}{rK} \tag{19}$$

---

[3] Comparing (17) and (19) one derives the equation:

$$q = T(\bar{y})/[1 - P(\bar{y})]$$

whose right-hand member involves only one endogenous variable, the productive capacity $\bar{y}$. This equation should not be interpreted as showing that capacity is determined by Tobin's q and nothing else. Indeed, q is also an endogenous variable, as appears clearly from (19). Although using a different explanation, namely the presence of adjustment costs, the literature on the q theory of investment derives similar simple relations between q and investment. Causal interpretations often given to these relations are no more justified than the one considered above.

which may be called Tobin's q, even though no reference is made to its evaluation by the stock market. The impacts are then defined by:

$$\frac{\delta c}{c} = \frac{\delta r}{r} - \frac{\delta w}{w} \tag{20}$$

$$\frac{\hat{\delta} q}{q} = \left[\frac{\delta p}{p} - \frac{\delta r}{r} \right] + \frac{wg(k)}{p - wg(k)} \left[\frac{\delta p}{p} - \frac{\delta w}{w} \right]. \tag{21}$$

Notice that (21) does not define the relative change of q, since this indicator also depends on the endogenous variables Ey, EL and K. In classical capital theory the relevant comparative statics properties do not involve the change in the value of capital but rather the impact that changes in quantities have on this value. Similarly here, the relevant properties do not involve the change of q but the impact that changes in prices and costs have on q.

For simplicity here we shall also assume $\delta h = 0$, i.e. changes in the expected value of demand Eu will be assumed to imply proportional changes in the standard deviation of demand. Differentiation of (17) and (18), F being assumed twice differentiable, then leads to:

$$a \left[\frac{\delta \bar{y}}{\bar{y}} - \frac{\delta Eu}{Eu} \right] + \frac{G}{T} \frac{\delta k}{k} = \frac{\hat{\delta} q}{q} \tag{22}$$

$$\frac{G}{T} \left[\frac{\delta \bar{y}}{\bar{y}} - \frac{\delta Eu}{Eu} \right] + \epsilon \frac{\delta k}{k} = -\frac{\delta c}{c} \tag{23}$$

in which a and ϵ are positive coefficients, which depend on the reference situation, and the argument $\bar{y}$ of G and T has not been written.

It is immediately clear from (22) and (23) that changes in expected demand do not react on capital intensity, but imply proportional changes of productive capacity.

Moreover, discussion of the values of the coefficients show that G^2/T^2 may be taken as small with respect to $a\epsilon$. It is then an admissible first approximation to say that capital intensity only depends on the relative cost of capital with respect to labour, the elasticity $1/\epsilon$ being equal to the product of the ex ante elasticity of substitution η and the share of the expected cost of labour in the expected total cost. This is the familiar relationship.

It is also an admissible first approximation to say that, for a given state of demand, productive capacity depends only on profitability, or rather on the impact of price and unit costs on profitability. The elasticity then is:

$$\frac{1}{a} = \frac{Eu}{\bar{y}} \cdot \frac{h[1 - P(\bar{y})]}{f(\bar{y})}$$ (24)

$f(\bar{y})$ being the derivative of F evaluated at $u = \bar{y}$. This elasticity tends to zero when the degree of uncertainty h decreases to zero. Discussion of equation (24) also shows that the elasticity is likely to decrease quickly as profitability q in the reference situation improves, this property applying for nicely behaved distributions. In other words, one can conclude that, for productive capacity to be sensitive to changes favouring profitability, uncertainty of demand must be significant and profitability low.

6. Comparative statics: the linear demand curve

Let us then take a kind of opposite to the kinked demand curve, namely a linear demand curve, leading to the following linear marginal revenue function:

$$R(y, u) = b\left(1 - \frac{y}{u}\right).$$ (25)

b is positive and equal to the price obtained for y close to zero, whereas the quantity demanded at a zero price is equal to $2u$.

The short-term decision then is given by (7) and the following form of (8):

$$\hat{y} = t(k) \cdot u$$ (26)

where $t(k)$ is the mark-up ratio that would be obtained at $y = 0$:

$$t(k) = \frac{b - wg(k)}{b}.$$ (27)

Similarly (9) implies

$$\bar{u} = \frac{\bar{y}}{t(k)}.$$ (28)

It follows that G and T given by (13) and (12) then only depend on $\bar{u}$.

Reflecting on the relevance of this linear case for macroeconomics, it is worth noting that the short-term decision implies the following price for output:

$$p = \frac{1}{2}(b + wg) \qquad \text{if } u \leqq \bar{u};$$

$$p = b\left(1 - \frac{\bar{y}}{2u}\right) \qquad \text{if } u \geqq \bar{u}. \tag{29}$$

Either the state of demand, as given by u, is such that there will be excess capacity (and the price then depends only on the wage rate and on b, not on the precise level of the state of demand u, for fixed $\bar{y}$ and k), or this state of demand is so favourable that capacity will be fully used and the price will be 'what the market can bear', i.e. it will not depend on the wage rate. I consider such a short-term flexibility of the price charged as unrealistic. This is one of the main reasons why I prefer to concentrate my attention on the case of the kinked demand curve, which is less commonly considered nowadays.

Let us, however, go on and consider the form taken here by the first-order conditions (10) and (11), namely:

$$[b - wg(k)] V(\bar{u}) = rk \tag{30}$$

$$- T(\bar{u}) g'(k) = \frac{r}{w} \tag{31}$$

where the function $V(\bar{u})$ is defined by:

$$V(\bar{u}) = \int_{\bar{u}}^{\infty} \left(1 - \frac{\bar{u}}{u}\right) dP(u). \tag{32}$$

One notes the formal similarities with equations (17) and (18) applying in the case of the kinked demand curve. There is, however, a significant difference. Equations (30) and (31) determine $\bar{u}$ and k rather than $\bar{y}$ and k. Of course the relation (28) shows that one easily goes from $(\bar{u}, k)$ to $(\bar{y}, k)$, but one may suspect that comparative statics properties are less simple. Let us further note in passing that the relation between $\bar{u}$ and $\bar{y}$ is easily visualized (see figure 7.2 where the solid straight line and the dotted line respectively represent $R(y, \bar{u})$ and $R(y, u)$ as functions of y).

For comparative statics properties two types of change of the demand curve must be considered. A shift δEu of the expected value of u means a change in 'the size of the market'. On the

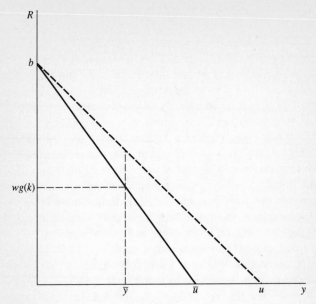

Figure 7.2

contrary a positive δb means a proportional increase in the price that can be charged at each level of output. Differentiation of (30) and (31) for a fixed coefficient of variation h eventually leads to:

$$\frac{H}{V}\left[\frac{\delta \bar{y}}{\bar{y}} - \frac{\delta Eu}{Eu}\right] + \frac{G}{T}\frac{\delta k}{k} = \left[\frac{\delta b}{b} - \frac{\delta r}{r}\right]$$

$$+ \frac{(1-P)wg}{rk}\left[\frac{\delta b}{b} - \frac{\delta w}{w}\right] \tag{33}$$

$$\frac{G}{T}\left[\frac{\delta \bar{y}}{\bar{y}} - \frac{\delta Eu}{Eu}\right] + \left[\epsilon - \frac{GV}{T^2}\right]\frac{\delta k}{k} = \left[\frac{\delta b}{b} - \frac{\delta r}{r}\right]$$

$$- \left[1 - \frac{GVwg}{Trk}\right]\left[\frac{\delta b}{b} - \frac{\delta w}{w}\right] \tag{34}$$

in which $H(\bar{u}) = 1 - P(\bar{u}) - V(\bar{u})$ and the arguments of the functions have not been written.

Comparison with (22)–(23), applying in the case of the kinked demand curve, is interesting. One first notes that changes in the size of the market act in the same way: they do not react on capital intensity and imply proportional changes of productive capacity.

In the left-hand side of the equations, the coefficients outside of the main diagonal are the same in (33)–(34) as in (22)–(23). On this diagonal the coefficient of δk is somewhat reduced, but (32) shows that V should be small, so that the change has little effect. However, the coefficient of $\delta \bar{y}$ has a completely different expression from (24). Like the coefficient a in (22), it is, however, an increasing function of its argument for nicely behaved distributions. Again, the effect of profitability on capacity is small except in cases where uncertainty of demand is significant and profitability is so deteriorated that $\bar{u}/Eu$ is unusually small. Similarly, it is found that the product of the coefficients of the main diagonal are likely to dominate G^2/T^2, so that the approximation stating that, for a given state of demand, capacity depends only on profitability and capital intensity only on relative costs may still be considered as valid.

This interpretation, however, takes it for granted that, in the right-hand side of the equations, one still finds the impacts of price and unit cost changes, respectively, on profitability and on the relative cost of capital with respect to labour. This is not exactly so, the right-hand side of equation (34) is not exactly equal to the change $- \delta c/c$ of the relative cost, as defined by (20). The impact of the change of the wage is somewhat reduced. This is easily explained: when the wage rate increases, $\bar{y}$ and k being kept fixed, the impact is partly transmitted as an increase in the price charged for output, as shown by (29); hence a relative increase in w is a little less inducing to capital–labour substitution than an equal relative decrease of r.

The right-hand side of (33) also is less easily interpreted than that of (22). Whereas the latter was clearly the impact on profitability, the coefficient multiplying the relative change of the real wage has no obvious meaning in the present case. We note that, in view of (17), the right side of (33) would be precisely equal to $\hat{\delta}q/q$ in the case of the kinked demand curve. Indeed, this form of the right-hand side applies more generally to any specification of $S(y,u)$, as can be seen by differentiation of (10).

With the linear demand curve, one can compute the value taken by q, as defined by (19), and find:

$$q = \frac{(b-wg)}{rk}\left[T - \frac{1}{2}(G+H)\right]. \tag{35}$$

The impact of changes of b, w and r on q, while $\bar{y}$ and k are kept fixed (but the impact on $\bar{u}$ is taken into account), may also be computed as being:

$$\frac{\hat{\delta}q}{q} = \left[\frac{\delta b}{b} - \frac{\delta r}{r}\right] + \frac{2TV}{T+V}\frac{wg}{rk}\left[\frac{\delta b}{b} - \frac{\delta w}{w}\right]. \tag{36}$$

It is easy to see that the coefficient multiplying the last bracket is usually much larger in the right-hand side of (33) than in (36). (As long as excess capacity occurs with a high probability, as $\bar{y}$ and k are fixed, changes in w are, to a large extent, transmitted to the price p.) Moreover, trying to define a 'marginal q' does not seem to help. The conclusion then is that, for computation of a relevant indicator of 'the impact of profitability', one should refer to the expression given by the right-hand side of (33) rather than to any direct measure of profitability.

7. Concluding remarks

A summary of the results was given in section 1. It will not be repeated here; but one may now be in a better position to reflect on the interest of the model and of its treatment.

Its main purpose was the derivation of some comparative statics properties induced by the behaviour of firms. These properties are relevant within a fuller discussion of the likely impacts of macroeconomic policies, wage policy in particular. But then other elements have to come into play, the formation of the demand for goods being the most important one. Although favourable to profitability, wage restraint is likely to depress demand. Whether it helps to stimulate the creation of new productive capacities or not depends on which of the two effects dominates. Similar remarks would apply to other policy issues. In other words, I see the model as one of the main building blocks of a larger system intended for the study of the medium-term equilibrium. This is the reason why the conclusions of this paper are intermediate products to be used in more embracing theories of the type studied by Tinbergen in the thirties.

The value of the model of course depends on its realism. To judge it, one may first wonder whether the specification is the proper one: what should one think about the relative importance of the features that it represents and of those that it neglects? Are the hypotheses about technology, markets and behaviour satisfactory as a first approximation?

One may also want to confront the model to data. The difficulty then is that expectations are assigned a major role, concerning both the level of demand and the profitability of production. At present we have hardly any data on medium-term expectations of business firms; we have to infer these expectations from past evolutions, an inference that is subject to errors. Two types of tests are nevertheless conceivable and have been applied on French data. The first one directly considers the first-order equations, such as (17)–(18), or more simply the equation deduced from them in the footnote that follows their presentation. I tried to apply this idea in Malinvaud 1986 and 1987. The second type of test was provided by P. Artus (1984) who fitted on macroeconomic time series a dynamic investment model inspired by the static model of this paper. I shall not surprise any econometrician when saying that the tests, although not negative, cannot yet be considered as fully conclusive.

References

P. Artus (1984), 'Capacité de production, demande de facteurs et incertitude sur la demande', *Annales de l'INSEE*, 1984.

J. Drèze (1979), 'Demand estimation, risk aversion and sticky prices', *Economic Letters*, 4, pp. 1–6.

F. Hayashi (1982), 'Tobin's marginal q and average q: A neoclassical interpretation', *Econometrica*, 50(1), pp. 213–24.

L. Johansen (1972), *Production Functions*, North-Holland, Amsterdam.

E. Malinvaud (1986), 'Jusqu'où la rigueur salariale devrait-elle aller? Une exploration théorique de la question', *Revue économique*, 37, pp. 181–205.

(1987), 'Capital productif, incertitudes et profitabilité', *Annales d'économie et de statistique*, 5, pp. 1–36.

T. Negishi (1979), *Microeconomic Foundations of Keynesian Macroeconomics*, North-Holland, Amsterdam.

J. Tinbergen (1938), *Les fondements mathématiques de la stabilisation du mouvement des affaires*, rue de la Sorbonne, Paris.

(1942), 'On the theory of trend movements' (first published in German), in L. H. Klaassen, L. M. Koyck and H. J. Witteveen (eds.), *Jan Tinbergen – Selected Papers*, North-Holland, Amsterdam, 1959.

J. Tinbergen and P. de Wolff (1939), 'A simplified model of the causation of technological unemployment', *Econometrica*, 7.

J. Tobin (1969), 'A general equilibrium approach to monetary theory', *Journal of Money, Credit and Banking*.

H. Yoshikawa (1980), 'On the "q" theory of investment', *American Economic Review*, 70, pp. 739–43.

Index